THE TREASURES OF JESUS

Alan Robinson

the TREASURES of JESUS

A Meditation on the Sermon on the Mount

ST PAULS

Cover design by Mary Lou Winters

ST PAULS
Middlegreen, Slough SL3 6BT, United Kingdom
Moyglare Road, Maynooth, Co. Kildare, Ireland

© ST PAULS (UK) 1994

ISBN 085439 466 4

Printed by The Guernsey Press Co. Ltd, Guernsey, C.I.

ST PAULS is an activity of the priests and brothers of the
Society of St Paul who proclaim the Gospel through the media of
social communication

CONTENTS

INTRODUCTION

The Sermon on the Mount (Matthew, Chapters 5-7) is a record of some of the sayings of Jesus of Nazareth. It is probably one of the most revolutionary documents ever produced. If the teaching of the Sermon were ever actually put into practice throughout the world, then the world would be completely changed into a happier and more peaceful place.

The Sermon has been described as the essence of Christianity. To some extent this is true, though it consists of ethical teaching rather than Christian doctrine. It is a description of the quality of life expected of those who live in the kingdom of God in the here and now.

These three chapters in Matthew's Gospel contain Jesus's teaching in his own words, as far as can be claimed, bearing in mind the various processes of transmission. Jesus spoke mainly in Aramaic, but the oldest version of the Sermon Christians have is written in Greek. This has been translated into English and so we have at best a third hand version of the Sermon. Then there is the question of when the sayings were first written in this form. As far as is known Jesus did not leave any written records, so his teaching is believed to have been oral. However, the disciples would be taught to memorise what their Master said, so it is likely that the Sermon is quite close to what Jesus actually taught. Much of the material was probably in poetic form when originally spoken, and this would make it easier to remember.

There is a smaller collection of similar sayings in Luke's Gospel, sometimes called the Sermon on the Plain (Chapter 6:20-49). Other similar material lies elsewhere in Luke. It may be deduced then that Matthew's collection has been put together by disciples, probably after the death and resurrection of Jesus. The whole Sermon may have come to Matthew in its present form, or Matthew may have had a hand in arranging the material.

This does not mean that Jesus did not give a sermon on a hill. He probably preached in many and varied places. There may have been a special memory of a particular time when he delivered some of this teaching in the form of a sermon to a large crowd of disciples. However, it is not certain that the Sermon as we know it was preached by Jesus in that exact form.

The Sermon is basically about the quality of life in God's kingdom:

(a) It starts with a number of beatitudes or blessings. These are the reward of those who belong to the kingdom (5:3-10). This is followed by several verses of general comment (5:11-16).

(b) Jesus then gives a new interpretation of the old law of Moses, but confirms its importance (5:17-48).

(c) This is followed by some practical advice on how to live in the kingdom, with comments on true religion and wisdom teaching mainly in the form of proverbs (6:1-7:12).

(d) Finally, there is a challenge to those who wish to be citizens of the kingdom in the form of several parables which spell out the discipline and dedication that are required (7:13-27).

Most commentators conclude that the rules of the Sermon are very difficult to keep. However, ideals exist to help people to try for perfection, even if in this life they cannot always reach it. Surely it is better to aim high and achieve much, than to aim low and achieve little.

1

Seeing the crowds, he went up on the mountain, and when he sat down his disciples came to him. And he opened his mouth and taught them, saying: **Blessed are the poor in spirit, for theirs is the kingdom of heaven.**

Chapter 5:1-3

This is the first of a series of beatitudes or blessings. The section is written in Hebrew poetic style. In other words, there is a certain resemblance to the psalms of the Hebrew Bible (that is the Old Testament). In these sayings Jesus seems to be promising that certain groups of people will receive a reward from God. The first group appears to be a strange one. What does it mean to say that a person is "poor in spirit"? It is difficult to argue that the phrase refers only to the poor in the worldly sense. This is not the language of ordinary life. Of course, we know what it means to say that a person is poor. But poverty of spirit is obviously something different. This is a good example of the difficulty of much religious language, which is often symbolic. To give a different sort of example: when we say that Jesus is the light of the world we do not mean that he is a light in the same sense as a lantern is a light. We know that we mean something else. Similarly, when Jesus talked about poverty of spirit he was not directly referring to money or worldly goods. However, the trouble with symbolic language is that there are often several ways to interpret the symbols. So how can we interpret this rather mysterious saying?

Someone who is immersed in a life of prayer would probably recognize that there are times when an awareness of one's deficiencies is overpowering. Isaiah, for example, when he had his wonderful vision of God in the temple, was overcome by a sense of his own unfitness to be God's prophet. His immediate reaction to the holiness and purity that he had encountered was to say, "Woe is me! For I am lost; for I am a man of unclean lips, and I dwell in the midst of a people of unclean lips; for my eyes have seen the King, the Lord of hosts!" (Isaiah 6:5). At that moment, Isaiah was poor in spirit. He felt completely inadequate. But in that same moment he was at the door of the kingdom of heaven. Do people feel like that today sometimes, not just very holy people, but ordinary folk? Many people in fact have this sort of experience. For example, a person might walk into a huge cathedral like St Peter's in Rome. His or her immediate reaction might be to feel very inadequate in the face of so many centuries of holy prayer in that place. At that moment that person may feel as inadequate as Isaiah did. However, the important point is that such an experience often goes with a person and he or she is blessed by a new insight into God's nature.

When the kingdom of heaven is mentioned, of course, there is a difficulty in understanding the symbolism. What is the kingdom of heaven and does it have a geographical location? The answer to the latter part of the question is fairly obviously negative, at any rate in relation to the earthly meaning of the word "geographical". Many people would agree that in this life the kingdom of heaven is within us in some sense, but at the same time we can also "give it" to other people and bring them into the kingdom. So the words seem to refer to a form of spiritual awareness, a knowledge that God is King of the Universe. Again this can be carried with a person wherever he or she goes. Heaven can be where a person is at any particular moment. This is not just for special people: it is for every single person who breathes. The breath of the Spirit is as free as the air in the atmosphere.

At the same time God is also King in another dimension for which we use a piece of shorthand, that is, the word "heaven". Consequently, people who experience poverty of spirit may subsequently have a very rich spiritual experience in this life. But also they may carry the hope in their hearts of having a future life in heaven with Christ. It is a

[handwritten margin note: Kingdom of heaven]

wonderful help in difficult times to believe that one day we shall actually be with Christ in heaven. The Rev. Sidney Smith once wrote jokingly that heaven might be like "eating pâte de foie gras to the sound of trumpets". Some people, of course, try to find a sort of heaven by using drugs. There may, indeed, be some kind of initial ecstasy, but the terrible experiences that some people have had surely show beyond doubt that drugs lead to hell, rather than heaven. The fact is, any attempt to create heaven upon earth must be a pale shadow of what heaven is really like. Any human speculation on the nature of heaven will probably fall far short of the truth.

Bible readings

Psalm 51; Isaiah 53; Mark 14:32-42.

Prayer

O Father, when we feel that you are far from us, help us to know you are with us in the wilderness of despair, help us to remember your suffering on our behalf and help us to see that the gateway to your kingdom is always open to us whatever our situation. Through the power of your Holy Spirit and through the grace of your Son, Jesus Christ, we pray that you will abide with us always. Amen.

2

Blessed are those who mourn, for they shall be comforted.

Chapter 5:4

Most people at some time in their lives suffer the loss of a loved relative or friend. Such an experience can be devastating and often involves a great testing of our faith in God. "Why has God allowed this to happen?" we may say. "If God really loves me he would not hurt me in this way."

Those who have been through such an experience may later find the wisdom and spiritual understanding to comfort someone else who is in a similar position. Quite often a friend or a close relative has this terrible experience of bereavement. It is never easy to find the right words and it is so easy to sound trite. We may remind the person we are trying to comfort of the Christian hope of resurrection or we may talk about the mysteries of God's purposes.

However, at the time of bereavement a person cannot usually think rationally about the deep wound which has been sustained. What that person needs, of course, is a lot of love from those around. At the same time, within the suffering of such a time people may feel close to Christ. While the temptation may be to become bitter, those who turn to Christ often find comfort at a very deep level. This has been tested time and time again in everyday life. It is not simply a pious hope. Christ is a living reality. He can be as close as a husband or wife, or as a brother or sister.

One person in the Bible who experienced a terrible bereavement was the Virgin Mary. We know little about her life after the death of Jesus, but we can imagine the depth of her sorrow and then the peak of her joy when the resurrection happened. Thinking about Mary's experience may help a person who has suffered a similar loss. What must it have been like for her to know that her son was also God's Son, and then for him to die as a condemned criminal? Few of us have an experience quite as devastating as that.

It is possible that this saying of Jesus has an additional symbolic meaning. People sometimes mourn for other reasons than the loss of a loved one. For example, as we grow older we may regret the loss of our physical powers, or mourn for the passing of a particular stage in our lives. The man who used to be an athlete may be confined to an armchair in a home for senior citizens. The woman who was once a great beauty may have to learn not to be admired quite so much as before. Here again the Bible may be helpful because the perspective of the Bible is a future one. The experience of heaven in the afterlife will replace in a wonderful way whatever has been lost in this life. Not only will lost loved ones be restored to us, but also we can hope for a quality of life which is surely happier than any happiness we have experienced on earth. This is not pie in the sky. It is a realistic Christian viewpoint. At the same time, we should always be thankful for the gifts of this life, which are many and varied.

At a different level we may learn to mourn any unhappiness we have caused other people. This is akin to repentance, and part of the process of repentance is being genuinely sorry for any hurt inflicted on others. For example, if we have had a hurtful quarrel with an old friend or with a member of the family, the process of turning to Christ can be very positive. Through Christ, people who have been divided can be brought together again. However, it is necessary to accept with humility the grace of God in his forgiveness of our failings. This also means that we must ultimately forgive ourselves, as well as each other, when we have done all we can to make amends.

Bible readings

Psalm 42; John 14:18-31; 1 Corinthians 15:51-58.

Prayer

O gracious God, comfort us in times of sorrow and sustain us in times of difficulty. We know deep in our hearts that nothing can separate us from the love of Christ. In him we offer ourselves to you with all our problems and all our difficulties. Please grant that your light may shine upon us this day and always, through Jesus Christ, our Lord. Amen.

3

Blessed are the meek, for they shall inherit the earth.

Chapter 5:5 (see Psalm 37:11)

This saying appears to contradict our daily experience. By and large it is not the meek who are in charge of the earth. Nor is it the meek who are usually in charge of most human ventures. The people in charge are usually the rich and talented. Moreover, our society values a modified form of aggression which fights to reach the top in any field of endeavour. This is not only applicable to work, but also to leisure activities. An ambitious person who becomes the boss of a department is admired, even if his methods are a little shady. The tennis player who loses well is not admired as much as the winner, even if he or she has won with a lot of swearing and an exhibition of bad manners. What, then, does Jesus mean by this saying?

The same word, here translated "meek", is used elsewhere in Matthew. In Chapter 11, verse 29, the Greek word is translated as "gentle":

Take my yoke upon you, and learn from me; for I am gentle and lowly in heart, and you will find rest for your souls.

It is certain that the word "gentle" is not to be taken in an over sentimental way. We know that the character of Jesus was anything but soft. Consequently, great self control and discipline appear to be involved in being meek and gentle in the Christian sense. For example, a very strong man who can hold his own in a fight and perhaps has a hot temper, can be meek and gentle with children. He puts aside both his physical power and his temper to be meek and gentle. But if it came to defending those children from an attacker he would no doubt use all his power and determination to achieve his aim.

Matthew also uses the same word in Chapter 21, verse 5, which is a quotation from the Greek Old Testament:

Behold your king is coming to you, humble and mounted on an ass...

This quotation from Zechariah 9:9 is a prophecy about a future king which Matthew takes to refer to Jesus. The key word in the quotation is translated "humble". The ideal king, then, God's Messiah, has this quality of meekness.

If we accept that Jesus was "meek" and yet strong, we can see that he and his followers have in some sense already inherited the earth. The people of the Church are God's representatives upon earth and eventually good will overcome evil. In our everyday lives things do not always seem to be arranged that way, but Christ has already won the battle against evil and it is up to this followers to strive to do the same. When we do so strive we are not battling with our own strength alone, but with the strength of Christ within us. Sometimes the battle is to be meek and yet inwardly strong in the face of the brash and bullying ways of the world.

From the above comments, it seems that meekness is a Christian virtue, part of the discipline of being a follower of Christ. This does not mean that we should not try to win at tennis. Nor does it mean that we should not encourage people to do well in their chosen professions. However, it does mean that in all our relationships, including those of leisure and work, we should cultivate a discipline of meekness and humility when these are appropriate.

Bible readings

Psalm 131; 1 Corinthians 13; James 1:9-20.

Prayer

O Lord, King of heaven and earth, who sent your Son in humility to show us the way to order our lives, please grant that we may follow Jesus in all that we think, or speak, or do. Especially help us to be meek and gentle with our neighbours, but at the same time to be strong to defend the weak. We ask this in the name of your Son, Jesus Christ, our Lord. Amen.

4

**Blessed are those who hunger and thirst for righteous-
ness, for they shall be satisfied.**

Chapter 5:6

H unger and thirst are basic needs which are essential
to life. To hunger and thirst after righteousness is
to express a basic need which is part of the spiritual life. This is made clear in both the Old and New
Testaments. Amos said that worship separated from goodness was not at all acceptable to God:

> ...to the melody of your harps I will not listen. But let
> justice roll down like waters, and righteousness like
> an everflowing stream (Amos 5:23-24).

If Amos were alive today he would certainly have plenty
to say, but his message would probably be essentially the
same. It's all very well for people to go to church on
Sunday all dressed up for the occasion, but what God is
equally interested in is what we have done about the needs
of the people in the Third World.

Of course, it is God who is righteous, and human beings
can merely try to achieve a measure of righteousness. However, the gift of God's grace does help. St Paul makes that
abundantly clear in several of his letters:

> For in it (the Gospel) the righteousness of God is
> revealed through faith for faith; as it is written, "He
> who through faith is righteous shall live" (Romans
> 1:17).

Abraham was made righteous through God's grace and
not by any action of his own. God said to him: "...walk
before me and be blameless" (Genesis 17:1).

Paul and Abraham were separated from each other by almost two thousand years and we are separated from them by thousands of years. Yet, their message is absolutely spot on for today. The person who has Christ as a daily companion will receive God's grace. That grace will transform even the worst parts of all of us.

At the same time, even in New Testament days there was disagreement as to whether a person could be righteousness through his own efforts. James's Letter appears to argue that personal effort helps:

Show me your faith apart from your works, and I by my works will show you my faith (James 2:18).

Common sense is often a useful guide in any dispute. It seems sensible to suppose that anyone who has faith in God will try to do good rather than evil. It is true that in every day life many pressures are working on us and these may "bend" our decisions. We may feel we want to do something to help the family round the corner, but fear of offending them may prevent us from acting. Yet, by and large, our intentions are often good and sometimes these are carried through!

Common sense also suggests that a person who does not believe in God may make a morally righteous decision. Each of us knows somebody in that category. We may have a friend at work, who is not interested in Church or the Bible, but he is a very decent person and does as much as the next man to help those who need help.

At the same time, God's righteousness is so far above anything human beings can aspire to that we can never boast before God in anything that we have done. Even those who have lived very saintly lives, like St Francis or Mother Teresa, can only do what they have done because of God's gifts to them. Moreover, each of us has to face the righteousness of Christ on the cross and at that point of realisation we can only wonder at the generosity of a God who can accept such suffering on our behalf.

Christians are on a pilgrimage through life and one of the aims of our pilgrimage is to try to live close to God, or like Abraham, to walk with God. Day by day we learn more about what attempting to be righteous involves for us. Through reading the Bible and through interaction with other people our experience grows, but above all it is in prayer that we come face to face with God's righteousness. By daily contact with God through specific prayer times and through the intermittent prayer that accompanies us through the whole day, we learn more about ourselves in relation to the almost unbearable brightness of God's righteousness. And in that learning we change and develop. What this means for you may be different in practical terms from what it means to someone else. We all start from different points, though we may aim to end up in the same pilgrim city. Whatever gifts and talents you have, it is part of the pilgrimage to use these for the good of humankind. Righteousness is a shared quality as well as being a personal one. God's righteousness is "good in action", as well as being a quality of his character. Any righteousness we may acquire is of little value if is not shown in active goodness.

Bible readings

Psalm 9:1-10; John 16:4-15; Romans 12.

Prayer

O Father, we kneel before you, trembling at the mystery of your presence, dazzled by the light of your glory, awed by the purity of your righteousness. Help us nevertheless to draw closer to you and to strive in our daily lives to do only what is acceptable in your sight. We ask this, in the name of your Son, Jesus Christ, and through the power of your most Holy Spirit. Amen.

5

Blessed are the merciful, for they shall obtain mercy.

Chapter 5:7

Mercy is very close to Christian love and to show mercy to enemies is close to the idea of forgiveness. A closely connected word in the Greek refers to the giving of alms, which implies showing mercy to those in need. Again, this is close to the idea of loving one's neighbour. Being in a position to grant mercy indicates some form of power. This power could be that of the judge who operates on behalf of society. In certain circumstances he might feel that mercy instead of severe punishment was appropriate. For example, a woman who was tempted to steal had been deserted by her husband. The judge took this into account and also the woman's previous good character. Instead of sending her to prison he showed mercy and placed her on probation.

On the other hand, the person with power could be someone who had been wronged by a friend. Ought he to show mercy to his guilty friend by forgiving him? A man finds his best friend and partner in business has stolen from the till. However, the friend shows that he is truly sorry. The wronged partner forgives his friend and their friendship is even closer than before. There is a certain parallel here to the petition in the Lord's Prayer: "Forgive us our trespasses as we forgive those who trespass against us."

The promise of Jesus is that those who show mercy will in turn receive mercy, presumably from God. This could be an indirect reference to the judgement we meet when we arrive in the next dimension of life. The idea of a final judgement is, in fact, older than Christianity. The ancient Egyptians had the idea that there was a moral judgement after death. Of course, it could be that God may show mercy to people in this life, though this is difficult to prove.

Unhappily some good people seem to suffer unjustly. Take the example of the woman who led a normal life up to the age of ten and who was then struck blind. She may feel that life has treated her very unfairly. However, the judgement of the after-life must surely put such injustices right. By the same token, the man who has had the power to oppress people in his care by putting them into prison unjustly and torturing them will surely have to explain himself to the Almighty on the Day of Judgement.

In the Old Testament the "mercy seat" was above the ark of the covenant in the temple. This was symbolic of God's forgiveness and his atoning love. Indeed, the Hebrew word used for "mercy seat" is from the same root as the word for atonement. The Hebrew people before the time of Christ had worked out a theology of atonement, which involved a concept of God's merciful forgiveness. Consequently, there is an interesting development from Hebrew thought into Christian thought. Christians believe that it is through Christ that God brings atonement, potentially to everyone. God's mercy through Christ's atoning work on the cross is free to all who accept Christ as Lord.

We do at times need to distinguish between mercy and justice. If we have to deal with naughty children, for example, we may find in some circumstances that some form of punishment is better for the child's development than leniency. The child who has been warned three times about bullying weaker children and is still being a bully, probably needs a sharp lesson. So mercy has to be thoughtful. On the other hand, mercy and love working together make up a combination which should be the first thought of a Christian in most situations. The good parent will learn by experience when to be lenient and when to punish. He or she will know when the punishment is enough. At the same time he or she will always be wise enough to know that love should be at the centre of family relationships. After all, where would we be without the mercy and love of God?

Perhaps the story in the Bible which most aptly illustrates the idea of mercy is the story of the prodigal son. The father of the prodigal son showed mercy to the young man when he returned home penniless. The brother was less merciful in his thoughts but did not have the power to do anything else but grumble. This is a wonderful parable about God's love and mercy towards us. If we take this parable and the Sermon on the Mount seriously, then we too ought to try to be merciful in our relationships.

Bible readings

Psalm 57; Mark 5:25-34; Letter to Philemon.

Prayer

Father in heaven, we earnestly ask that you may so fill our hearts and minds with the spirit of your love, that our first thoughts may be to show mercy rather than to act severely, to show forgiveness rather than to seek revenge, to show generosity rather than to display meanness. We ask this in the name of your Son, Jesus Christ, our Lord. Amen.

6

Blessed are the pure in heart, for they shall see God.

Chapter 5:8

In this verse the word "pure" refers to spiritual or ethical purity. Essentially this means having pure motives for our actions. If a man says he wants to work for a charity because he wants to help people, though his real motive is to impress his employers, that would be an impure motive. On the other hand, if a man tells his dying father that he will recover, his motive may be pure, even though he has told a lie. It is what is in the heart that counts with God.

Matthew uses the word elsewhere to describe the purity of physical objects. This is especially interesting in Chapter 27, verse 59, where the shroud used for the body of Jesus is described as clean (pure). In Chapter 8, verses 2-3, the allied verb is used to describe the cleansing of a leper.

The physical sense is used as a metaphor for the spiritual sense in a saying about the Pharisees (23:25-26). Jesus castigates the Pharisees for washing the outsides of cups and plates while the insides "are full of extortion and rapacity". This saying shows the importance to the Pharisees of ritual purity, but Jesus is emphasizing that such outward actions are useless unless the heart is pure. The same is true of Christian baptism. If an adult receives outward baptism but does not truly repent, then the baptism is not doing what it was intended to do.

How can a person try to acquire purity of heart without being hypocritical? We have to be true to the inner meaning of the Christian law, but at the same time we have to be true to ourselves. There has been some confusion in Christian circles about the nature of purity. It has often been confused by the idea that some normal bodily functions are allegedly impure. This, of course, is untrue except where the body is misused. The human body is a beautiful creation. Physical love within marriage is beautiful and essentially pure. That is one aspect of being true to ourselves. But to sleep around is not being true to the best self, to the self that God is creating in each of us.

Being true in the ethical sense means having loving motives in all our actions. This does mean keeping the basic moral laws as listed, for example, in the Ten Commandments. However, it might be necessary in certain circumstances to break a commandment to keep the true spirit of the law. If John kills the man who is trying to rape his (John's) mother, though murder was not the intention, then John might be trying to keep the true spirit of the law. John loves his mother and knows inwardly that it is his duty to honour and protect her. Whenever the true spirit of *agape* (Christian love) is lost, even the moral law cannot guarantee our purity. St Paul understood this very well:

> For the law of the Spirit of life in Christ Jesus has set me free from the law of sin and death (Romans 8:2).

Those who are pure in heart will be privileged to see God. The word used for "see" is often used of "seeing with the mind". That is the case in Matthew at Chapter 9, verse 2, where Jesus is described as seeing the faith of the people bringing a paralysed man to be cured. We often use the word see when actually we did not "see". For example, we might say to a friend, "I see you were at Jim's last night", when actually we *heard* our friend was at Jim's.

In a similar way this saying of Jesus in the Sermon refers to a mental perception of God. That is not to say that people do not have special visions. Isaiah, for example, saw a vision of God sitting on his throne (Isaiah 6:1). Some people are privileged to have unusual experiences, though often they do not like to talk about them. Often such experiences involve some perception of God being with us, as when a man who has lost his wife is strongly aware of a comforting presence; or sometimes an experience of God comes when a person perceives something beautiful in nature like a snow covered mountain or the first star of the evening in a deep blue sky.

To see or know God must be wonderful, however it occurs. What Jesus is saying is that Christians who are trying to lead a good life will have a perception of God's presence in their hearts and minds. The Sermon on the Mount does emphasize at many points the importance of the true, inner experience, over against the outward trappings of religion. This is not to condemn ceremonies and rituals. They are designed to help people to have an experience of God. However, unless the outward actions are accompanied by the genuine pulses of the spirit, then they will be in vain. The person who worships every Sunday but cheats his neighbour every Monday is performing the right outward actions in church; but his immoral actions belie the prayers and worship he has taken part in before God and in the presence of the Christian community. It is only when our actions match our outward words to God that we are approaching anything like purity of heart.

The well known hymn by John Keble illustrates this saying of Jesus very well. The last verse reads:

> Lord, we thy presence seek;
> May ours this blessing be;
> Give us a pure and lowly heart,
> A temple meet for thee.

Bible readings

Psalm 24; Jeremiah 31:31-34; 1 Peter 1:13-25.

Prayer

O God, Father of our Lord Jesus Christ, who showed us the true way to achieve purity of heart, we beseech you by that same Jesus Christ, who is our Saviour and Preserver, to guide our thoughts in purity that we may become truly your children, that we may stand without shame before the glorious light of your presence. Amen.

Blessed are the peacemakers, for they shall be called sons of God.

Chapter 5:9

J esus also said, "Peace I leave with you; my peace I give to you; not as the world gives do I give to you. Let not your hearts be troubled, neither let them be afraid" (John 14:27).

In the Sermon on the Mount Jesus seems to be referring to people who bring good and happy relationships between people and nations. For example, somebody who brings a quarrelling couple together by using tact and diplomacy could be said to be a peacemaker. However, in John's Gospel Jesus seems to be talking about an inward, personal peace. That sort of peace of mind is possessed by people who live close to God in everyday life. In fact, these two meanings do have an obvious connection, because the person who possesses the peace of God inwardly is surely the sort of person who would be an agent of peacemaking.

In Hebrew and Arabic the concept of peace includes prosperity and well being brought about by God's blessing. Unfortunately life is not always fair and the peaceful person may not be gifted with worldly goods. However, he would have a deep consciousness of well being and he would have God's blessing in the spiritual sense. Every day would seem to that person be full of blessings all waiting to be counted.

It is a Christian virtue to be a peacemaker. If there is a squabble of some kind, whether it is between individuals or nations, then Christian love in action should be able to make a contribution to solving the problem. Unfortunately, the people involved do not always wish to know about the message of peace and love because they are too worked up about things to care. The whole aim of the participants may be to gain victory at any cost. Take the example of two people who quarrel because they both covet promotion in the same firm and each is jealous of the other. In those circumstances a Christian who knows of the situation can do at least three things. He can first of all try to mitigate any damage to personal relationships that may be caused. Secondly, he can pray that peace will come. Thirdly, he can wait for an opportunity to try to bring about peace, if he has any power to act.

Of course, if people are practising the Christian life, then prevention should be more appropriate than cure. In a Christian community, peace should prevail. Disagreements may occur, but these should be settled peaceably. If there are continuously warring factions in a church group then all of those involved are failing in the Christian vocation. Too often there are squabbles about why things didn't go exactly as planned or about who should have done what. Perhaps people should pray more often together, not only in public worship, but in smaller groups.

The true reward of the peacemaker is to be a child of God and, therefore, a brother or sister of Christ. That is a wonderful thought. This saying of Jesus can, of course, be turned round. If we believe we *are* children of God, then we should be peacemakers. The difficulty can be, of course, that there is a fine line between peacemaking and interfering. Nevertheless, it is worth making the effort even if we are not always popular. At the same time, the antidote in most difficult circumstances is a good dose of unsentimental Christian love.

Bible readings

Psalm 34; 1 Samuel 24, Ephesians 2:13-22.

Prayer

O God, may your peace reign in our hearts and may we be agents of your peace wherever we may be. Help us in all circumstances to strive to keep your word and to be loving, generous and welcoming to all the people we meet in the pilgrimage of life. Grant that the peace of Christ may dwell within us and that your Holy Spirit may guide our every thought. We ask these things in the name of Jesus Christ, our brother and our Saviour. Amen.

8

**Blessed are those who are persecuted for righteousness'
sake, for theirs is the kingdom of heaven. Blessed are you
when men revile you and persecute you and utter all
kinds of evil against you falsely on my account. Rejoice
and be glad, for your reward is great in heaven, for so
men persecuted the prophets who were before you.**

Chapter 5:10-12

Jesus himself knew something about being persecuted
even before the dreadful events of Holy Week. There
are various levels of persecution. Sometimes people
are victims of verbal abuse. Those who belong to minority
ethnic groups in this country are unfortunately often subjected to this sort of unkindness. Racism is a recurring
problem throughout the world. Jesus himself took much
criticism and abuse from establishment figures who were
jealous of his success with the Jewish people. He dealt with
such attacks by the use of parable and by showing clearly
the motives of his enemies. The parable of the vineyard is a
good example of this. In this story Jesus showed that the
messengers sent by the owner of the vineyard (the prophets
of ancient Israel) were persecuted by the stewards of the
vineyard, and that even the son of the owner (Jesus himself) was killed by the greedy tenants (see Mark 12:1-12).

At the other end of the scale martyrdom was always a
possibility for early Christians, St Stephen being the first
recorded person to give his life for Christ. No doubt Jesus
knew this when he taught his followers beforehand how
they should react. Some people had to accept physical
abuse as well as verbal abuse. St Paul is a good example.
He, of course, had persecuted the very first Christians, but
later he too had to submit to beatings and stonings for the
sake of Christ.

Martyrdoms are not unknown in modern times. Christians in certain South American countries in their pursuit of the freedom of Christ have paid the supreme penalty because of their faith. Most people, however, are not asked to face such a test. Yet, any Christian may be subjected to some sort of persecution. Sometimes this can be sarcasm about religion in general. At other times it can be more pointed criticism of the Church and its members by people who do not really understand the nature of the Christian faith. Nevertheless it is a worthwhile witness to make people aware that we are Christians, whether we meet them at work or in some club or society.

Jesus is clear that the reward of the persecuted Christian is to be in God's kingdom, not only here and now, but also in the next life. He also makes the point that people of God before his own time suffered persecution. He particularly singles out the prophets as a group of people who were God's servants but were nevertheless persecuted by their fellow countrymen.

Jeremiah is an example of a suffering servant of God. He preached an unpopular message, that is, the fall of Jerusalem and the defeat of the nation by a foreign power. Many thought he was a traitor and he was treated accordingly. He was ostracized, banned from his priestly vocation, isolated from his family, ridiculed and even thrown down a well and left to die. Fortunately he was rescued and lived beyond the catastrophe. At that time he was able to testify to God's love and forgiveness when his countrymen were in dire straits:

...for I will forgive their iniquity, and I will remember their sin no more (Jeremiah 31:34).

If we should be subjected to persecution of some kind what ought we to do? Suppose a group of people we happen to be with suddenly attacks the Church and all it stands for rudely and with some personal force. It is always tempting to hit back and in some circumstances it may be necessary at least to respond verbally, though hopefully in a reasoned way. Perhaps we should always be armed with the best arguments to defeat the devil. Sometimes, of course, people genuinely seek to know the truth and we should be prepared at any time to explain our faith to those who are puzzled. In any case, testimony to our faith should surely have a measure of priority. But such testimony, of course, could be the silent, though effective, protest of turning the other cheek. Have we got the courage to stand with Christ whatever the circumstances?

Bible readings

Psalm 70; Jeremiah 15:15-21; 2 Corinthians 11:24-31.

Prayer

O God our Father, help us to be faithful to our Christian vocation in all circumstances. If we are put to the test please give us the strength to bear our troubles, in the sure knowledge that Christ himself is walking with us. If we are persecuted please guide us in our behaviour so that we may uphold the honour of the Church. We ask this through our Lord and Saviour, Jesus Christ. Amen.

9

You are the salt of the earth; but if salt has lost its taste, how shall its saltness be restored? It is no longer good for anything except to be thrown out and trodden under foot by men.

Chapter 5:13

The expression "salt of the earth" seems to have attained a permanent place in the English language. We generally use the phrase to refer to some group of people who make a vital contribution to society as a whole. We might, for example, say that British miners are the salt of the earth – and with some justification. By this description we might mean that British miners have courage, tenacity and grit. A further implication would be that Britain would be a poorer place without them.

There are many phrases that the English language has borrowed from the Bible. Sometimes the meaning changes in everyday parlance. After all, language is growing and changing constantly. However, when we are trying to fathom the meaning of a Biblical phrase we may have to put aside the modern meaning temporarily, in order to look at the given phrase through unprejudiced eyes.

What did Jesus mean by this saying? A look at the use of a word in the Old Testament is often illuminating. The Israelites used salt for ceremonial purposes and particularly talked of a covenant of salt to indicate an unbreakable covenant (Numbers 18:19). An Arabic word related to the Semitic word for salt means "covenant". This may mean that when salt had been shared in a meal, then the participants were in a state of peace with each other. Mark quotes Jesus as also saying, "Have salt in yourselves and be at peace with one another" (9:50). Some scholars associate saltness with wisdom, but usage seems rather to support the idea of salt being symbolic for peace and concord between individuals or groups of people.

One aspect of Jesus's intention may then refer to his followers being agents of peace and love in the world. At the same time the idea that salt improves the taste of food is very strongly stated. Christians, then, could be the element in the world which gives meaning or value to the whole of society. Without the peace and love of the Gospel the world would indeed be tasteless. Imagine life without daily contact with Christ! Yet some people have not yet received this wonderful gift.

Additionally, Christians are the inheritors of the covenant with God through Christ and as such have the responsibility of filtering the love they have in Christ throughout the whole of society, just as salt flavours the whole of a dish. Jesus also used the idea of yeast in bread to show how a small group can influence the world. Our Lord was very down to earth. He certainly didn't live in an ivory tower, and perhaps we shouldn't either.

We can now return to the modern meaning of the phrase "salt of the earth". This, too, should surely be applicable to the Christian community. Followers of Christ may well have courage, tenacity and grit in the way they remain loyal to Christ and in the way they carry out their vocations as disciples of Christ. Our thoughts lead us, then, to the idea that Jesus is calling his followers to be people of character who are going to change the world. They cannot do this alone, but only by the grace of God and within the fellowship of Christ. This is not simply an ideal. Unless it is a reality of daily life it doesn't mean much. Also, it's of no use saying, "I can't do anything because I'm only one person. What influence can I have?" The fact is that each of us can influence events just a little. Just as ants can do wonders when all their efforts are added together, our individual efforts are very important. Some little action or word of ours may have untold influence.

Bible readings

Psalm 26; John 15:12-17; 2 Thessalonians 1.

Prayer

O God, we know that you create us anew each day and that you sustain us in all that we do. We pray that you will give us grace to be the salt of the earth, courage to fight for God's kingdom and constancy to remain true to our calling. We ask this in the name of Jesus Christ, our Lord. Amen.

You are the light of the world. A city set on a hill cannot be hid. Nor do men light a lamp and put it under a bushel, but on a stand, and it gives light to all in the house. Let your light so shine before men, that they may see your good works and give glory to your Father who is in heaven.

Chapter 5:14-16

C hristians accept that Jesus is the Light of the World in a very special sense. However, in this saying, Jesus is explaining to all of his followers that they must also be lights in the world. Of course, we cannot be the main beacon light, because that is the function of Jesus. At the same time each of us can be a little beacon lit by his love. That may sound pretentious, but the fact is that every time our Christian calling guides us to help somebody else and every time we openly confess our faith to our non-Christian friends, we are shining a beam of Christly love into possibly dark places.

Jesus goes on to say that a city set on a hill cannot be concealed. Generally speaking a city was built on a hill in ancient times in order to provide a good defensive position and also to have a clear view in every direction. God's city on earth, David's city of Jerusalem, is just such a city. It is also clearly visible for miles and in a sense acts as a spiritual beacon for the many pilgrims who go there. Some towns and villages in Britain are so placed in prominent positions that they act as a social and often a spiritual focus for a whole area. This is particularly true of many cathedral cities. For example, Lincoln Cathedral is visible for miles in every direction.

Jesus continues with a homely parable about an oil lamp and a bushel measure (a kind of tub). It would obviously be fairly silly to light a candle or an oil lamp to hide it under a tub. To use a modern analogy, we don't switch on a table lamp and then put it under the table. The function of the lamp should be to provide light for everyone in the house. We, then, should not hide our Christian faith. We should show by the good things that we do that we are following in our Master's footsteps. Not only that, we should be giving glory to God by testifying to the spiritual power that lies behind the whole universe.

Jesus also indicates that not only is God his Father, but also that God is our Father. This is further shown in the Lord's Prayer which comes later in the Sermon. If God is creator of all that is, and if he is sustaining his creation, then there is a very real sense in which every baby that is born is given its thought and being by God. We are beginning to learn more about the physical side of our being because of the greater scientific knowledge we have. But the intrinsic nature of our being, our spiritual nature, is still very much a mystery. However, even a child can understand what it is to say, "Father", and to be able to address God in this way is a wonderful gift for all of us.

Light is very important as a symbol in many religious faiths. Hindus, for example, have their Festival of Light, Diwali; and Jews have a similar festival called Hanukkah. In poetry and religious belief light often stands for goodness as opposed to darkness and evil. From this saying, therefore, we may deduce that Christian love and goodness are in contrast with the various evils which plague our world. The powers of light are at war with the powers of darkness. No individual can escape from this struggle, nor from the responsibility of making moral decisions. Most human beings seem to be a mixture of light and darkness, just as the social scene is a mixture of good and evil. Each of us has to struggle with the darker side of our nature from time to time.

Sometimes life seems very dark, with storm clouds swirling all around. This can happen to each individual. For example, when a man loses his job, or a woman loses her mother who has had a painful struggle before passing over, life can seem very bleak indeed. At these times it is difficult to shine as a light of Christ, but nevertheless it is at such times when the light of Christ may shine in us. If we can overcome the darkness within us, then our faith can help those around us who may also be suffering. In addition to these individual times of darkness, life can sometimes be dark for a whole group of people, even a nation. Take for example, a time when a country is devastated by terrible storms or floods. Then indeed lights are needed to help people to survive. True, practical help is vital, but spiritual help is also vital at such times. If even one individual can bring the light of Christ to the whole group, then the morale of everyone may climb dramaticatily. That is what is needed above all, hope and faith in the future.

Christians have to shoulder their responsibilities by responding to Christ's call to bring a little light into this sometimes very dark world. Everything we do is important and our whole orientation is even more important. If our lives are spent in the light of Christ then we may have the grace and power to carry our little lamps into the dark places around us.

Bible readings

Psalm 139:1-18; John 3:16-21; 1 Thessalonians 5:1-11.

Prayer

To you, O God, we owe all that we are and ever shall be. Fill us with the light of your Holy Spirit that we may be your lights in this dark world. May the light of Jesus guide us on our path and may your holy word be a lantern before us as we walk our pilgrim way. We ask these things through your Son, our Lord Jesus Christ. Amen.

11

Think not that I have come to abolish the law and the prophets; I have come not to abolish them but to fulfil them. For truly, I say to you, till heaven and earth pass away, not an iota, not a dot, will pass from the law till all is accomplished.

Chapter 5:17-18

It is useful to think of the Transfiguration story when pondering on the meaning of this saying. The three closest disciples, Peter, James and John, were privileged to see Jesus with Moses and Elijah. Moses, of course, symbolized the Torah or Law, while Elijah symbolized the prophets (Matthew 17:1-8). This vision occurred immediately after the declaration by Peter at Caesarea Philippi that Jesus was the Messiah (Matthew 16:16). The vision not only emphasises the continuity of God's revelation, but also the validity of the law and prophecy in relation to the new era that Jesus inaugurated. The Transfiguration story, then, whether it is interpreted literally or symbolically, seems to confirm Jesus's words in the Sermon in a very mysterious way.

The Jewish law as expressed in the Old Testament is valid for Jewish people today. For example, the idea of kosher or acceptable food depends on definitions given in the Old Testament. At a deeper level, Jewish people revere both the Ten Commandments and the summary of the law in the two great commandments. To Christians, however, some of the laws in the Book of Leviticus, for example, seem to be out of date. But the laws which Moses first presented to the Israelites, that is the Ten Commandments, are still regarded as valid by most Christians, though some would argue that the law of Christian love supersedes all other laws. Jesus himself, however, as we shall see later in the Sermon, combined a reassertion of the value of the

Decalogue with a deeper interpretation of the moral commandments, an interpretation which searched the hearts of his disciples by concentrating on human motives. Laws only help to define sin: the causes of sin lie in the heart and mind.

According to Jesus the word of the prophets was also still valid, and he (the Messiah) had not come to abolish their work. While there are various facets to the work of the Old Testament prophets, there are certain key ideas which the major prophets have in common. God's judgement and God's salvation are two such ideas. Even in the Book of Jeremiah, essentially a work describing God's judgement, there are hopeful sections which preach salvation (see Jeremiah 31:31-34). Conversely, in the work of Second Isaiah (Chapters 40-55), who was essentially a prophet of hope and salvation, there are assumptions about God's judgement (see Isaiah 40:1-2). It is fairly clear that part of the work of Jesus was (and is) to express God's judgement of the world, but at the same time to bring about God's salvation of the world. Theologians like St Paul would not have been able to understand this unless the prophets had earlier explored such concepts. Even Paul's great statements about justification by God's grace alone would not have been possible if Paul had not been steeped in Old Testament ideas. It is clear that God's revelation included a lot of preparatory groundwork by the prophets.

It is also quite clear then that Jesus saw himself as the fulfiller of the work of Moses as a law giver and of the work of the prophets as God's messengers. Moreover, the theologians of the New Testament expanded our understanding of Jesus's work as the Messiah. The four evangelists, for example, show how Jesus was a suffering Messiah, thus fulfilling the Suffering Servant prophecies in the Book of Isaiah (see Isaiah 53). Yet again, the author of the Letter to the Hebrews explains clearly the atoning work of Jesus, basing his ideas on the Jewish Day of Atonement (see Hebrews 9).

Bearing in mind also that the coming of the Messiah

was foretold by some of the Old Testament prophets, this shows a unity in the Bible as a whole which is surprising when it is remembered that many different writers in different centuries contributed to it. If Moses produced the first written "document" (at least the Decalogue) of those making up the Bible in the thirteenth century B.C. and if the last documents of the New Testament were produced in the second century A.D., then the processes of writing and editing the biblical documents must have taken about fifteen hundred years. Presumably that is a short time in God's time scale, but to us it is a vast period of time. Indeed, God does move in mysterious ways.

Bible readings

Exodus 19-20; 1 Kings 19:9-18; Matthew 16:13–17:8.

Prayer

O God, our Father, we thank you for the wonderful revelation that you have given to us through many people and over many centuries. Help us to understand more clearly the nature of your law and your love. Give us wisdom also to understand the work of your prophets. But above all grant us the grace so to pray that we may come closer to our Lord and Saviour, Jesus Christ. Amen.

12

**Whoever then relaxes one of the least of these command-
ments and teaches men so, shall be called least in the
kingdom of heaven; but he who does them and teaches
them shall be called great in the kingdom of heaven.**

Chapter 5:19

There seems on the surface to be a contradiction in
this saying in relation to what Jesus says elsewhere
about the legalism of the Pharisees. When the disciples were plucking ears of corn on the Sabbath day the
Pharisees were very critical. Jesus uses their own method
by quoting a story from the scriptures which tells how
David and his men ate the sacred bread in the temple. Then
Jesus hammers home his point with the wonderful saying,
"The sabbath was made for man, not man for the sabbath;
so the Son of man is lord even of the sabbath" (Mark 2:
27-28).

Some scholars argue that Matthew's Gospel is a book
with a strong Jewish interest and that it is Matthew himself
who is emphasizing the importance of the law. To some
extent this is true and it is frequently difficult to separate
the ideas of the evangelist from the events he is describing.
Yet in the Sermon on the Mount we have a collection of
Jesus's teaching which has a very strong claim to be the
authentic word of Our Lord. Much of the material also
appears in Luke's Gospel, so it is not simply Matthew's
views that have to be considered (see, for example, Luke
11:33-36 and 12:22-31). So what does the saying mean?

Jesus, in fact, makes the Jewish law more difficult by
highlighting the motives that lie behind sin, that is, anger,
greed, lust and hatred. Consequently, he seems to be arguing that the law must be kept in the heart and not just
outwardly. The whole tenor of the Sermon is about the true
law, God's law. At the heart of the divine law lies good-

ness. It would be a nonsense to argue that Jesus is giving approval for all time of some of the laws about ritual washing. For example, in the Book of Leviticus the whole of Chapter 15 is about cleanliness. These were just the kind of laws that the Pharisees took to extremes. If Jesus had gone to the same extremes that would contradict what he says, not only in other parts of the Sermon, but also in many passages throughout all the Gospels.

It is possible that Jesus is referring in this saying to the new law as outlined in the Sermon. This would be supported by the parable about the two houses at the end of the Sermon (7:24-27). The person who "hears these words of mine," he says, "and does them will be like a wise man who builds his house upon the rock" (7:24). Jesus himself was a teacher of the law, as were the Jewish rabbis. He is often addressed as Rabbi or Master. The Pharisees learned a trade, as Jesus did. (Note also that St Paul, an ex-Pharisee, was a tent maker by trade.) The Pharisees taught a group of twelve disciples, as Jesus did. Jesus used similar teaching methods to the Pharisees, as in the example given above when he quoted scripture. In other words, in many ways Jesus was a man of his own time. Where he diverged was in the aim and content of his teaching. It may be that he was criticizing the Pharisees in this verse (5:19) for teaching people to break the true law, the law of the heart.

Jesus's prescriptions for being great are in interesting contrast to the world's standards. In another place, for example, he says that greatness is associated with the humility of being a servant (Mark 10:43). It is this idea of service which has been so influential in the history of the Church, as in the work of people like Albert Schweitzer who gave up a successful career to work in a leper colony; or Leonard Cheshire, a war hero who became the servant of the physically handicapped. Of course, what such people are doing is keeping God's law of love. Yet again, Jesus makes the paradoxical statement, "...he who is least among you all is the one who is great" (Luke 9: 48).

In the context of the Sermon, however, a slightly different perspective is given. Greatness is ascribed to those who keep the law and teach it. Their greatness is defined in heaven, not upon earth.

To put this in another way, God regards human attempts to keep his law as important. This could refer to the law of love or to the laws of a good state. St Paul supports both of these ideas. In 1 Corinthians 13 he describes the importance of the law of love, but in his Letter to the Romans he recommends that Christians should obey the lawful authorities (Romans 13:1-4).

Of course, we must remember that Jesus, though very demanding, was also ready to forgive what would be regarded by the Pharisees as serious transgressions of the law. Perhaps the most famous example of this was when Jesus forgave the woman caught in the act of adultery (John 8:1-11).* According to Jewish law she should have been stoned to death. This story and the whole tenor of the Gospel show that God's forgiving love through Christ is at the very centre of the Christian message.

In modern times we sometimes separate the laws of the state from moral laws, though of course, there are many occasions when the two are interwoven. In many countries adultery is regarded by some people as a moral offence, but not as a transgression of the law of those countries. However, theft would be regarded in most countries as both an offence against the laws of the state as well as an offence against the moral law. On the other hand there could possibly be occasions when theft could be morally justifiable. Suppose a mother stole food to feed her starving children when she had no other way of obtaining food. Then we are in a very debatable area. Christians can at least turn to Christ for guidance when there are difficult decisions to make. The ultimate rule

---

* Note: the story about the woman caught in adultery does not appear in some ancient manuscripts.

then would be the golden rule of loving our neighbour as ourselves. If our decisions are guided by the true spirit of agape (Christian love), then we are surely not far from keeping God's law.

Bible readings

Deuteronomy 6:1-9; Psalm 19; Romans 7.

Prayer

O God, our Father, guide us in the way that we should go and show us what the right action is when we are in doubt. Place in our hearts a love and respect for your laws and give us the strength and wisdom to abide by the teaching of Jesus as far as we are able. In this and all things, we hope for the grace of that same Jesus Christ and we pray for the guidance of your Holy Spirit each day in our thoughts and deeds. Amen

13

For I tell you, unless your righteousness exceeds that of the scribes and Pharisees, you will never enter the kingdom of heaven.

Chapter 5:20

The scribes and Pharisees were the educated people among the Jews. St Paul was educated as a Pharisee:

I am a Jew, born at Tarsus in Cilicia, but brought up in this city at the feet of Gamaliel, educated according to the strict manner of the law of our fathers, being zealous for God as you all are this day. (Acts 22:3)

It is probable that in the time of Jesus the education of children and older students consisted largely of ethical and scriptural teaching. It is thought, however, that arithmetic was also taught. As the Jews spoke Aramaic at that time, those who wished to read the scriptures had to learn either Biblical Hebrew or Greek. The scriptures had been translated into Greek in Egypt in the third century B.C. Many Jews of the Dispersion (those living outside Israel) used the Greek version. There is evidence that Matthew knew the Greek text.*

It can be seen in St Paul's letters that Paul was a highly educated person, versed in Jewish and Greek culture. He

---

* Perhaps the most outstanding example which demonstrates this is where Matthew quotes the prophet Isaiah: "Behold a virgin shall conceive and bear a son, and his name shall be called Emmanuel" (Matthew 1:23). At Isaiah 7:14, the source of this quotation, the original Hebrew text uses a word meaning "young woman". The Greek translation, however, uses a Greek word (*parthenos*), which means "virgin". This is the version quoted by Matthew.

was brought up in the Greek speaking area of Cilicia. If he was typical of the Pharisees, as he seems to have been, then they must have been equally well educated. His knowledge of the Jewish scriptures was obviously very good and while he knew the Hebrew he was probably also familiar with the Greek Old Testament (now called the Septuagint).

The scribes and Pharisees did their teaching in synagogues and in the temple precincts. Jesus did the same. The recorded confrontations between Jesus and the Pharisees show that he could invariably defeat them in argument. A good example of this is given in the confrontation story where Jesus was challenged to say whether it was lawful to pay the Roman tax. His reply was the unforgettable, "Render therefore to Caesar the things that are Caesar's, and to God the things that are God's" (Matthew 22:21).

Jesus probably had a synagogue education as a child. It is recorded that he later read the scriptures in the synagogue (Luke 4:16-19) and, of course, his visit to the temple as a boy shows that he had great skill in discussion even then (Luke 2:41-51).

In this saying in the Sermon (5:20), it seems that Jesus condemned the ethical standards of the scribes and Pharisees. The scribes, in fact, were teachers of the law and many of them were Pharisees. Jewish law is a mixture of ethical, civil and criminal law. An approximate modern equivalent of a scribe is difficult to define. He had some characteristics of the lawyer and some of the preacher. However, despite the expertise of this group they often missed the point of the laws they were teaching. That, perhaps, is what Matthew is emphasising in his account of Jesus's Sermon.

To be sure, some scribes and Pharisees were enlightened enough to know that love of God and love of neighbour were at the heart of the law. It is recorded of Hillel, a famous rabbi who lived just before the time of Jesus, that somebody once asked him to explain the Jewish law briefly. He said he could do this while standing on one foot and he did so, quoting the Jewish text which says, "Love your neighbour as yourself" (Leviticus 19:18). Unfortunately, most Pharisees were hamstrung by tradition and could not escape from the minutiae of scriptural legalism. Not many Pharisees were aristocrats and some of them had a sympathy for the plight of the common people in relation to the law. Nevertheless, they were in a culture trap and were bound so tightly that they could not show too much leniency.

Jesus was able to cut through tradition as Alexander had cut through the Gordian knot. He saw clearly that people and not rules are what really matter. A good example of this was when he healed the man with the withered hand on the Sabbath day, thus shocking the scribes and Pharisees (Mark 3:1-6). It was the system Jesus was criticizing to a large extent. To his listeners he was really saying, "Yes, the law is important. I have just said so. But you must do better than the teachers of the law. God's righteousness is not like their righteousness. You must *really* love each other."

In the sayings that follow Jesus showed clearly what was wrong with scribal teaching.

Bible readings

Proverbs 4:10-19; 1 John 2:1-11; Acts 26:4-18.

Prayer

O Lord, Father, Son, and Holy Spirit, show us how to love others more than we love ourselves. Give us wisdom and understanding so that we may respect and keep your law. But at the same time help us to avoid hypocrisy and give us the spirit of loving tolerance that we may resist the temptation to condemn other people's failings. Above all, accompany us each hour of each day so that we may walk safely along the path to your kingdom. Amen.

14

You have heard that it was said to the men of old, "You shall not kill; and whoever kills shall be liable to judgement." But I say to you that every one who is angry with his brother shall be liable to judgement; whoever insults his brother shall be liable to the council, and whoever says, "You fool!" shall be liable to the hell of fire. So if you are offering your gift at the altar, and there remember that your brother has something against you, leave your gift there before the altar and go; first be reconciled to your brother, and then come and offer your gift. Make friends quickly with your accuser, while you are going with him to court, lest your accuser hand you over to the judge, and the judge to the guard, and you be put in prison; truly, I say to you, you will never get out till you have paid the last penny.

Chapter 5:21-26

In this saying Jesus examines the sixth Mosaic commandment.* The majority of people, including those without any religious faith, would agree that it is wrong to kill another person. Jesus extends the prohibition to holding anger in the heart against someone. It is true, of course, that many people do become angry from time to time. Jesus himself was angry sometimes, but his anger was always a righteous anger. What he seems to be condemning here is the nursing of anger so that it becomes permanent, perhaps even obsessional. This kind of anger or resentment can exist within the family, at the work place or even within the Church community. Grudge bearing is the antithesis of Christian forgiveness and unhappily this attitude sometimes appears in Church life.

It is significant that Jesus implies that God will not find offerings in worship acceptable when the worshipper has an

---

* There are different ways of numbering the commandments. To some people this will be the fifth commandment.

outstanding quarrel with his neighbour. The quarrel ought to be settled before true worship can take place. Quite frequently Jesus criticizes those who practise outward religion while at the same time failing to love their neighbour. Purity of heart before God is not a matter of practising the correct rituals. It lies deep within us and any hatred will pollute the Spirit's love which grows within our spirits.

Perhaps the main point that Jesus is making here is that the motive behind a killing is the cause of the action. This, of course, is well known among the writers of crime fiction. How often does the fictional detective examine the motives of his suspects? Actions are like plants in a way. Just as a plant has roots, so an action often has hidden causes. The followers of Jesus should examine their own motives and feelings and if they recognize anger within themselves, then they should perceive the danger signals. It has to be remembered, of course, that there are other motives for killing than anger. Greed for someone's possessions is often a motive. Jealousy also can motivate to kill, but jealousy is closely akin to anger. The existence of other motives for killing than the one mentioned by Jesus does not mean that Jesus's Sermon is incomplete. The whole message of the Sermon is that unworthy motives lead to serious sin. What Jesus is doing is giving a selection of examples.

We may sometimes feel that anger is justified. Certainly, anger in the cause of righting an injustice against a defenceless person could be justified. However, that anger should be channelled into right action and should not grow into personal resentment. Take, for example, the man who is indignant because his child has been unjustly treated by a teacher at school. His anger might get out of control to such an extent that he used physical violence on the teacher concerned. It is fairly clear to most of us that there are better ways of dealing with the problem, though action would certainly be necessary. However, if representations at the school were not effective, the anger might be more likely to build up into violent action. The person trying to follow the advice of Jesus would obviously attempt to avoid any violence and would try such peaceful methods as were necessary to achieve his aim. As a last resort he might go to court.

Jesus is quite clear that judgement will follow transgressions of the true moral law, which is of the heart. Of course, actions like killing must be subject to very serious judgement. But Jesus goes much further. He also condemns the wickedness held inside us. Equally he condemns the angry or insulting word. It is easy to see that beating up a person because of his race is wrong, but to use insulting racist language would also be condemned by Jesus.

Taking life in other contexts may reflect more complex motives. Abortion and euthanasia are two examples. In either case there may be a worthy motive behind the action. For example, an abortion might be justified if the mother's life were in danger or if a young girl had been raped. Euthanasia, some people might argue, would be justified when a person was to all intents and purposes living the life of a vegetable. However, in either case, reverence for life should be taken very seriously and the commandment not to kill applies in either case. While the Sermon does not deal with these problems directly, yet again, we have to accept the principles behind the Sermon as guidelines for our thinking in other problem areas. Love for God and love for neighbour are paramount.

It is interesting to note that the language of the law courts is used in this passage of the Sermon. The offender will go before the judge and may be sent to prison. Undoubtedly this is intended to be a parallel for God's judgement. The divine judgement is inexorable. The last penny will be paid by those who do not obey the moral law.

Some people may well point out that good people quite often suffer hardships while law breakers sometimes prosper. This problem was recognized in ancient times by Jeremiah:

Why does the way of the wicked prosper?
Why do all that are treacherous thrive? (Jeremiah 12:1)

This phenomenon is not only a problem for religious belief. It is also a logical problem. The evident injustice is usually resolved by appealing to a higher court. In other words all injustices experienced in this life will be rectified in the world to come.

Most of the higher religions postulate a future judgement. Certainly, in the two religions most closely related to Christianity, Judaism and Islam, the idea of a divine judgement after death is very strong. Christianity also places a strong emphasis on this aspect of belief. However, this is balanced to some extent by the doctrine of the atonement. At the day of judgement, it is hoped, Jesus will stand beside us and plead our case. Nevertheless, it would be a very foolish person indeed who did not take God's judgement seriously. The Sermon is a very hard hitting document and every Christian should read it with care because it contains some of Our Lord's central teaching.

Bible readings

1 Kings 21:1-19; Psalm 1; John 5:19-29.

Prayer

O God, we know that your nature is love, but yet in our hearts we have not love. We deserve judgement, O Lord, but please bring us not to what we deserve, but lead us to the peace of a clear conscience, that we may be made righteous through the grace of your Son, Jesus Christ. Amen.

15

You have heard that it was said, "You shall not commit adultery." But I say to you that every one who looks at a woman lustfully has already committed adultery with her in his heart. If your right eye causes you to sin, pluck it out and throw it away; it is better that you lose one of your members than that your whole body be thrown into hell. And if your right hand causes you to sin, cut it off and throw it away; it is better that you lose one of your members than that your whole body go into hell.

Chapter 5:27-30   (see Matthew 18:8-9)

The seventh Mosaic commandment* is here scrutinized by Jesus. It can be imagined that those who actually listened to his teaching pricked up their ears considerably when adultery was mentioned. The punishment for infringing this law was death. How could Jesus disagree in any way with Moses on this particular question? Of course, Jesus only disagrees by saying that Moses had not taken the law far enough. Yet again, Our Lord recognizes that the inner motive is usually the cause of sin.

It is not possible to punish people in this life for what they think, not at any rate unless they state their thoughts in such a way that they break the law. Consequently, the punishment for sinful thoughts, according to this saying, is reserved for the next life where the punishment could be to go to hell. Of course, we have to recognize that Jesus was a first class teacher and that good teachers often exaggerate to make sure their points strike home.

It is difficult for us to come to terms with the idea of hell. The Bible nevertheless is quite clear that hell exists. Many other faiths take the same view. The Buddhist de-

---

* There are different ways of numbering the commandments. To some people this will be the sixth commandment.

scription of hell, for example, would frighten the most hardened sinner if it was understood literally. At any rate, to avoid the punishments of hell, according to Jesus, we should rid ourselves of the causes of the sin. Whether it is the eye or the hand that causes us to fall, we should sacrifice it for the sake of our eternal welfare. It is unlikely that Jesus intended people to take this invitation literally. Rather does he intend to show that real repentance is required. Accordingly, if we find ourselves looking at a member of the opposite sex with seriously improper thoughts, then we ought to change direction before the thoughts are carried into practice. We must remember, of course, that adultery involves sexual activity by a married person with someone other than the spouse. (The original Hebrew definition may have been somewhat narrower.) However, presumably Jesus was aware that people often have mixed reasons for their actions. In contrast to his statement in the Sermon, he did forgive the woman caught in adultery, as noted in a previous section (see John 8:1-11).

Adultery is only one of a number of sexual actions which may hurt other people. Jesus does not mention here gang rape, sex outside marriage, prostitution, sex with under age people, child abuse, perversions of various kinds, nor a number of other sexual activities. Here again we have to apply the general principles given in the Sermon and elsewhere in the Bible. If a sexual action is loving in the Christian sense, and is not likely to hurt other people, then it is probably morally right. Where there are problems, these ought to be resolved by the Christian within the parameters of Christian morality, and the principle guide should surely be love within Christ's love.

To return to the question of adultery, perhaps like Jesus we should be ready to forgive others, but for ourselves we should always take the commandment very seriously. We know that people sometimes feel forced by circumstances into extramarital relationships. Outsiders usually do not know the full story. The one who is unfaithful may have been treated cruelly by his/her partner.

Or the so called innocent partner may have been unfaithful in the past. Consequently, we should be very wary about condemning others. Yet we should not readily forgive ourselves for contemplating such a relationship outside our own marriages. We should think of all the hurt that can be caused to a number of people, with possibly disastrous consequences to any children involved. If children are left with only one parent, or if they have a step parent, then the normal loving relationship is broken, however loving the step parent may try to be. It is also well to consider what might happen to children with only one parent. It may be that they will be subjected to temptations which would not have come their way if their parents had stayed together. For this sort of reason as well as for the sake of their sacred vows, Christian people should surely try every conceivable means to avoid a marriage break up.

On the question of hell as a place of punishment, as previously mentioned, this is in the realm of symbolic language. Just as the word "heaven" is shorthand for a state following death, so the word "hell" is a similar piece of shorthand. We can, in some respects, be in hell or in heaven in this life. Either condition is a state of mind. So, whatever the parameters of the future life may be, the state of consciousness beings find themselves in may be heavenly or hellish. The writings of people like Dante portray a symbolic version of the future life. We do not actually know the exact conditions "there", and the Bible makes only very general statements about both hell and heaven.

One of the main points of this saying in the Sermon is to tell us that we must think now and again about ourselves and make some judgements. It is part of the Christian pilgrimage to endeavour to grow in holiness, to grow closer to Christ. There may be times when we have to be ruthless in casting out those things which are a hindrance to our development in the religious life. At the same time, we need to be realistic and should not try to overstretch our capabilities. Sometimes we have to live with ourselves as we are and hope that Our Lord will accept us with our many imperfections.

Bible readings

2 Samuel 11; 1 Corinthians 7:1-16; Matthew 1:18-25.

Prayer

O God, Father of Our Lord Jesus Christ, guide us with your Holy Spirit so that we may not sin in our hearts. Help us to grow closer to you each day and help us to be faithful in all our relationships. Grant that we may be able to live up to our ideals within the community of the Christian faith. Amen.

16

It was also said, "Whoever divorces his wife, let him give her a certificate of divorce." But I say to you that everyone who divorces his wife, except on grounds of unchastity, makes her an adulteress; and whoever marries a divorced woman commits adultery.

Chapter 5:31-32

In this saying Jesus is referring to the Jewish law concerning divorce. In Deuteronomy it is clear that a man could divorce his wife simply by giving her a certificate of divorce and dismissing her, though the law implies that he should do this only if he finds some "indecency" in her (24:1). The words translated "indecency" literally mean "nakedness of a matter", which is fairly vague. The word for divorce in both Matthew's Greek and in Deuteronomy means "dismiss" or "let go". The same word is used in the New Testament for releasing a debtor. It is clear that a woman did not have the same right to issue a divorce certificate.

Jesus says that a divorce should only be justified by "unchastity". This English translation softens the original Greek word which means "fornication". If a man should divorce his wife for any other reason, according to Jesus, each party would commit adultery if he or she married someone else. It can be seen plainly, then, that Our Lord wished to modify Jewish law by making divorce more difficult. At the same time, he insisted that the only ground for divorce should be adultery.

Jesus does make another statement about divorce, recorded in Matthew 19:3-9, where he says that when two people are married they have become one flesh. This is followed by the well known words, "What therefore God has joined together, let not man put asunder." Again, unchastity is given as the only justification for divorce. In

Mark 10:2-12, where the same story is told, Jesus says nothing about a justification for divorce. Interestingly, many people believe that Matthew had Mark's Gospel by him when he was writing his own Gospel. Did Matthew slightly alter the story in order to be consistent? Or did two people have different memories of what was said?

We may say to ourselves at this juncture, "What is the point of all this delving into the meanings of words written so long ago in other languages?" The fact is, divorce is such a critical matter, both for Christians and others, that we ought to know precisely what Jesus said on the question. It is quite clear that he viewed divorce as the breaking of a vow to life-long commitment. From Jesus's words the only ground for divorce would be adultery. Presumably we would wish to give women the same rights as men in our society, so a woman would also be justified in taking divorce proceedings on similar grounds. The question then arises, "What about all the other grounds for divorce allowed by our society?" Included in those grounds, there is the possibility of agreement that a marriage has broken down.

For a start we must agree that Christians do not have the right to force their views on other people who are not Christian. Then we have to ask whether Christians should follow the general trend in society in this and other matters. The fact is that relationships within marriage are so complicated that once compromises are made, then the moral problems become accordingly more complex. Some Christians may wish to stand by the statements made by Jesus and not allow divorce for themselves except for the adultery of the partner, or perhaps not even then. Other Christians may wish to think about the true spirit of the law, which is Christian love, and make any decisions in the light of their concept of such love. This may include forgiveness of the partner, or it may allow divorce on the compassionate ground that both partners are going to lead such an unhappy life that divorce would be the loving solution in the circumstances.

Jesus, of course, brings God into the equation in some of his sayings on divorce. He also gives importance to the idea that a married couple have become one flesh. Whatever conclusion we may come to, we must surely agree that Jesus thought divorce was a very serious matter. Consequently, whatever decision is made by Christian people in a discussion about a particular divorce, they ought to take it as seriously as Jesus did. If divorce is decided upon, even after such serious consideration and sincere prayer, then the people concerned have at least tried to come to a decision in the light of their faith.

The next step, once a decision to divorce is taken, must surely be to alleviate any hurtful consequences, especially for any children involved. This assumes that attempts to be reconciled have been made, but unsuccessfully. Christian consideration and love ought to be shown to each other by the divorcing partners. Too many divorces end in acrimony and less than elevating arguments about possessions. If possible, continuing friendship should be sought, with understanding and compassion, though with sensible limitations. Love for the children and a serious attempt to maintain family bonds should be important aims. If this sounds difficult, then it must be remembered that Christ should be in the middle of the situation. Of course, for a Christian couple, if Christ had been allowed into the situation in a realistic way from the beginning of the marriage, then the decision to divorce probably wouldn't have been take. At the same time, life unfortunately falls short of our ideals, so sometimes we are in the business of picking up the pieces of broken promises.

Bible readings

Hosea 6:1-6; Psalm 61; Colossians 3:12-25.

Prayer

We ask, O Lord, in times of difficulty, that you will give us wisdom and understanding to know what is right. Surround us with your love, O Lord, and help us to love each other as brothers and sisters of Christ. Give us patience and perseverance in love and give us a spirit of forgiveness that we may learn to forgive as we are forgiven. Amen.

17

Again you have heard that it was said to the men of old, "You shall not swear falsely, but shall perform to the Lord what you have sworn." But I say to you, Do not swear at all, either by heaven, for it is the throne of God, or by the earth, for it is his footstool, or by Jerusalem, for it is the city of the great King. And do not swear by your head, for you cannot make one hair white or black. Let what you say be simply "Yes" or "No"; anything more than this comes from evil.

Chapter 5:33-37

Perhaps Jesus is referring to the following saying from the Old Testament: "And you shall not swear by my name falsely, and so profane the name of your God: I am the Lord" (Leviticus 19:12). This reference shows that Jesus was as familiar with the Jewish law as any other Rabbi. But yet again he gives his own interpretation which must have been quite startling to his disciples.

Of course, in our society, as in ancient Jewish or Roman society, people do take oaths, for example, in courts of law or in marriage. We might prefer to call the latter a promise, but it is nevertheless a promise, either before God or before witnesses. Such oaths or promises are regarded as binding by law. However, people do break their promises or disregard their oaths, so in one sense Jesus might be warning us of the danger of taking oaths which later might be broken, perhaps because circumstances have changed.

It is possible that Jesus was referring mainly to private oaths or promises between two individuals. A good example of the former would be a vow to fast until something was achieved. In Acts of the Apostles a number of people vowed to fast until they had killed St Paul (see Acts 23:12). It is interesting to speculate how long the people who made the vow kept to their fast. An example of a promise between two individuals could be an agreement between partners in a business. They might well trust each other and not have a written legal agreement. One of the partners, however, might change his mind and break his promise. Probably most people would agree that it is better to undertake a proper business partnership from the beginning in those circumstances.

Then there is the question of marriage. Two young people might decide not to marry but to commit themselves to each other in a private promise. One is reminded of Juliet's warning to Romeo not to swear by the "inconstant moon". Would it be sufficient for two people in those circumstances just to say, "Yes, I love you"? Perhaps it would be better than making a promise which might later be broken. Or would it be wiser to undergo a ceremony before witnesses in order to show serious intent?

Jesus is actually challenging us to think before we undertake to do things. It's all very well to say, "Yes, I will be there on Monday. I promise." But can we keep the promise? Some people wisely add, "God willing." On many occasions when we lightly make a promise it would surely be better to say merely "Yes" or "No". Some religious groups would go further and refuse to take oaths in a court of law, arguing that their commitment to religion makes it unnecessary because they already tell the truth in all circumstances. Yet, they may make exceptions to their alleged code, because they may argue in some circumstances that it is better to lie to a person dying of cancer than to tell that person the truth. Again, there is the possibility of inconsistency.

We should certainly accept the challenge put before us by Jesus. We should think very carefully indeed before making a promise before God, especially if we are going to use God's name. To put the point in another way, we should not use God's name in vain. In that respect Jesus is surely agreeing with Moses. It would be wonderful if we could ask Jesus precisely what he meant by this saying, as his listeners in the first century could. As usual, we are left with our general knowledge of the teaching of Jesus together with our capacity to reason. Reason seems to say that oaths in courts of law or in legal agreements are precautions against making promises lightly. But reason also tells us that we should avoid taking oaths or making promises in circumstances where it is possible we might not be able to keep them.

Bible readings

James 5:12; 2 Chronicles 6:14-23; Hebrews 6:13-20.

Prayer

O God, may your word be in our word, and may our undertakings be made sincerely and wisely. Guide us in all we say and help us to keep any promises we make. Give us the grace not to use your name lightly, but only in the context of truthful intentions. We ask this through Jesus Christ, your Son, who brought us the Spirit of all truth. Amen.

18

You have heard that it was said, "An eye for an eye and a tooth for a tooth." But I say to you, Do not resist one who is evil. But if anyone strikes you on the right cheek, turn to him the other also; and if anyone would sue you and take your coat, let him have your cloak as well; and if anyone forces you to go one mile, go with him two miles. Give to him who begs from you, and do not refuse him who would borrow from you.

Chapter 5:38-42

This saying shows clearly the difference between the standards of those who are living in the kingdom of God compared with worldly standards. Jewish law provided for retaliation to the precise amount of the offence. This is sometimes known as the *lex talionis*, or the law of retaliation (Exodus 21:24). Some claim that this law was a safeguard against unfair revenge in prescribing the exact penalty. However, Jesus puts this law under scrutiny and questions its spiritual validity for those who are truly God's children.

It is clear that Jesus himself put this policy into practice when he allowed himself to be captured, condemned and crucified, having committed no offence other than to preach a gospel of God's forgiveness and forgiveness between enemies. His words of forgiveness on the cross (Luke 23:34) make the point more potently, because he was actually practising what had preached in a situation where it would have been more natural to curse his enemies.

Turning the other cheek is never easy and it sometimes leads to contemptuous actions from the oppressor. Spiritual strength in such a situation is often taken for weakness or even stupidity. Take the example of a man who refuses to pilfer from work as some of his colleagues are doing. First he is ridiculed. He smiles and takes the insults without complaining to the boss. The result is that even more insults are showered upon him.

Christians, it is hoped, would generally recognize a truly Christian action when they saw one. But many people reject God's kingdom, or perhaps have not been introduced to it. Standards of behaviour in business and in personal relationships can sometimes be ruthless. Opponents are cut down unscrupulously. This is also true in politics. The man or woman who offends against the party line is given short shrift and may be expelled from whichever party is concerned. This may happen even when someone is acting in good conscience. Over history there have been many people who have stood against the crowd, accepting insults without complaint. Their offence is usually that they have disagreed with some powerful group or other. John Bunyan is a prime example. He had to spend years in prison because he would not worship in the prescribed way. The result in his case, of course, was the glorious *Pilgrim's Progress*. Bunyan gained deep spiritual insights from the persecution he suffered.

How far do we have to go in following the philosophy of turning the other cheek? According to Jesus there is no limit. He says elsewhere, concerning the number of times one ought to forgive, "I do not say to you seven times, but seventy times seven" (Matthew 18:22).

In relation to Matthew 5:42, many people in all branches of human endeavour have high ideals and do care a lot for the under-privileged. For example, a firm which supports handicapped children is acting in the spirit of God's kingdom. So while there is much cruelty in the world there is also much kindness. People may not always recognize the fact, but the standards preached by Christ have affected our society in all sorts of ways. The kingdom of God sometimes grows underground and then shoots up where it is least expected. For example, not everyone who works for the Samaritans is a convinced Christian, but the work done by the organization is inspired by Christ himself in his most famous parable (see Luke 10:25-37).

Jesus says we ought not to refuse the person who begs or borrows. Many people, Christian or otherwise, do give to worthy causes, sometimes on a very systematic basis. This is surely in keeping with the Christian ideal. But there is also another kind of giving which responds to an actual situation need. This can be very difficult. Should money be given to someone who is immediately going to spend it on drink? This is an individual decision and it is difficult to legislate for all situations. The loving reaction which wishes to give immediately is one response and undoubtedly it would be in the spirit of what Jesus is saying. It is difficult to imagine that Jesus would ever turn anyone away. However, he would quickly spot the false claimant and give an appropriate response. It is a pity that we do not always have the wisdom to do the same. On balance it is surely better to respond with love and to help where possible.

It is given to few people to have the courage to take Jesus literally. St Francis and Mother Teresa are very much the exception rather than the rule. But perhaps the rest of us can take some inspiration from them. If we ponder on the teachings of Jesus we may find that we are moved to respond sometimes in the true way of his kingdom. Sometimes this can lead to embarrassment. If you decide to take a homeless person who is not very well dressed for a meal, the owner of the restaurant may want you out of his place as quickly as possible. Hopefully he won't actually insist you leave.

Bible readings

Genesis 45:1-15; Luke 15:11-32; 1 Timothy 1:12-17.

Prayer

O God, Father of our Lord Jesus Christ, by your grace enable us so to walk in the footsteps of your Son that we may live daily in your kingdom in anticipation of the day when we finally enter therein. Help us to be forgiving, to love those who hate us and to pray for those who may persecute us. Fill us with the spirit of Christian love so that all our actions may be performed in your service. Amen.

19

You have heard that it was said, "You shall love your neighbour and hate your enemy." But I say to you, Love your enemies and pray for those who persecute you, so that you may be sons of your Father who is in heaven; for he makes his sun rise on the evil and on the good, and sends rain on the just and on the unjust. For if you love those who love you, what reward have you? Do not even the tax collectors do the same? And if you salute only your brethren, what more are you doing than others? Do not even the Gentiles do the same? You, therefore, must be perfect, as your heavenly Father is perfect.

Chapter 5:43-48

I n this saying Jesus seems to be referring to the Jewish law, which demands love of the neighbour if he is one of the same group of people (Leviticus 19:18). Jewish law does not contain the statement that we should hate our enemies, though many passages assume that it is the natural thing to do. Take the following quotation from a psalm:

Arise, O Lord! Confront them, overthrow them! Deliver my life from the wicked by thy sword... May their belly be filled with what thou hast stored up for them... (Psalm 17:13-14).

However, Jesus suggests that enemies should be loved. In a sense the writer of the Book of Proverbs anticipates Jesus by advocating a similar approach:

If your enemy is hungry, give him bread to eat; and if he is thirsty give water to drink; for you will heap coals of fire on his head, and the Lord will reward you (Proverbs 25:21-22; see 24:29).

This suggests that practical experience shows that enemies can be more challenged by a loving response than by an angry one. But Jesus goes even further by demanding that we actually pray for our enemies. Our love for those who hate us should not be merely skin deep. Think about that for a moment. Suppose you were unjustly put into prison, "framed", as the expresssion goes. Suppose you also knew who framed you. Could you, while languishing in prison, pray for those who had put you there? That is the challenge.

One result of such loving treatment of our enemies is that we shall be true sons of God. God himself does not differentiate between categories of people. People who are unjust receive rain and sunshine in the same way as those who are just. Even the hated tax collector and the despised Gentile can behave in a loving way to those who love them. Christians are asked to do much more. They must strive for perfection.

It seems hard to suggest that we should try to be perfect like God. However, in a slightly different form, this demand is already in Jewish law:

> You shall be holy; for I the Lord your God am holy (Leviticus 19:2).

The same Greek word used by Matthew (translated "perfect") is used of physical development and can mean "mature" (see Hebrews 5:14). In the spiritual sense it has the meaning of "completeness" and is used not only in the Sermon but is also used in the Letter of James in the same sense:

> And let steadfastness have its full effect, that you may be perfect and complete, lacking in nothing (James 1:4).

In the Old Testament several people have this quality of completeness. Noah "was a righteous man, blameless in his generation; Noah walked with God" (Genesis 6:9). The word translated "blameless" literally means "made whole". Likewise, God said to Abraham, "...walk before me and be blameless" (Genesis 17:1). These two patriarchs were made whole because they walked with God. Therefore, if we walk with God and rely upon his grace, through Christ, we too may be made whole.

It may be that there is a blueprint for each of us, a plan for our perfected personalities which God already has in his mind. If we are aware of this we may be able to cooperate with the divine purpose. It is true that some Christians believe that we can achieve nothing without God's grace. But if God's grace is working in us, then it is God's perfecting power which is working in us and through us. In that sense, we may be healed, made whole and gradually drawn towards the pattern of Christ's perfect example of personhood. How far we can achieve this in the present life is an unknown quantity. However, as we believe in the afterlife it seems logical that the process of growing towards perfection in Christ should continue in heaven. We should never confuse this process with being over pious. Jesus, as he comes to us through pages of the Bible, was very down to earth, humorous and against pious platitudes. The description of the hypocrites at prayer later in the Sermon (6:5) is a good example of the robust way in which Jesus dealt with false piety.

Bible readings

1 Chronicles 28:9-10; 1 John 3:11-18; John 17:20-26.

Prayer

O God, our Father, we know we can only approach your perfect being through the intercession of your Son, Jesus Christ, the one perfect human being. Yet through him, our great high priest in heaven, we know that we have power to be made whole, so that the growth of our spirits may follow their true pattern in your creative plan for us. We pray, therefore, that each day we may walk with you in our imperfection that we may by your will reach the perfection of heaven. Amen.

20

Beware of practising your piety before men in order to be seen by them; for then you will have no reward from your Father who is in heaven. Thus, when you give alms, sound no trumpet before you, as the hypocrites do in the synagogues and in the streets, that they may be praised by men. Truly, I say to you, they have received their reward. But when you give alms, do not let your left hand know what your right hand is doing, so that your alms may be in secret; and your Father who sees in secret will reward you.

Chapter 6:1-4

The first sentence of Chapter 6 introduces a number of sayings which are warnings against hypocrisy. The Greek word for "hypocrite" usually refers to an actor, someone who is pretending to be something he is not. Of course, in the theatre that is the legitimate intention of the actor, but in religion pretence can be wrong – for example, if a person is acting a part in order to impress other people. Unhappily, Church people are often open to a charge of hypocrisy because they are imperfect. Their behaviour cannot always match up to the ideals in which they believe. That, however, is not what this saying is about. It is rather about those people, hopefully a minority, who deliberately cultivate an appearance of piety in order to massage their egos.

Matthew has Jesus using the word "hypocrite" frequently, usually to refer to the scribes and Pharisees. In one story some of this group come to Jesus and ask him a question about taxes, hoping to catch him out in some treasonable statement. As usual Jesus sees through their "play acting" or hypocrisy and tells them so in plain language (see Matthew 22:15-22). This, however, illustrates the universality of the sayings of Jesus. The message is applicable at all times and in all places. Yet, we should not be gazing around to see who the Pharisees in our midst are. We should instead be looking at ourselves to see if we have any "Pharisaic" tendencies.

The first saying of the section refers to the giving of alms. The Greek word used for "alms" also means "mercy". The motive in giving, then, is to show mercy or loving kindness to someone in need. It was customary to give to people on the street or outside the temple (see Acts 3:2). Non-Jews were sometimes noted as generous alms givers (see Acts 10:2). There was, however, a temple treasury to which people contributed as they went past (see Mark 12:41). Jesus was watching people beside the treasury one day and observed a poor widow placing a very small amount in the treasury. She received great praise for her generosity because what she gave was virtually all she had. Oddly enough, this story is in Mark and Luke but does not seem to be in Matthew (see Mark 12:41-44). Here again we see the universality of the message. We should not be too ready to criticise what other people give, but rather we should be challenged ourselves to consider whether we are giving in the same proportion as the poor widow.

Those who deliberately give large amounts of money in order to impress people are given ironic treatment by Jesus. It as if they had a servant walking in front of them, blowing a trumpet and announcing the generosity of the giver. Or to put that in a modern context, it is as if a person advertised on television that he was giving a hundred pounds a week to Oxfam. People like that do receive a reward though, which is that they are noticed; but it is an empty reward, for the opinions of men are of little value if God disapproves of what they do. Then Jesus uses a very powerful metaphorical saying: "Do not let your left hand know what your right hand is doing." This surely means that, when we give, we should do so with the determination not to allow our egos to be inflated by our own generosity.

It is an interesting thought that God knows all that we do anyway. If we give secretly, in such a way that the amount we give is not known by anyone, nevertheless God knows and he will reward people in his own way. What the reward is we are not told. However, even at the human level we do need to satisfy our own consciences that what we give is appropriate.

Our society is organized in such a way that there are many avenues for giving. Giving to the Church, if we are churchgoers, would no doubt be a priority. Over and beyond that there are numerous causes to which we could contribute. Appeals are constantly being made and it is very difficult to decide which causes are the ones to support and certainly this needs careful thought. Some people prefer systematic giving. Others prefer to give as the spirit moves them. At certain times in our lives we may not be able to give very much because of family or other commitments. At other times we may have more freedom to give. It is really impossible to give precise advice in such a personal matter. Each individual's conscience must be the guide.

Bible readings

Proverbs 19:17; Acts 3:1-10; 2 Corinthians 9.

Prayer

O God, giver of all good things, we thank you for the generous gifts you have given to us. Even to be part of your creation is a most wonderful gift and we pray that all peoples may be able to share equally in the bounty you have provided. To this end, give us generous hearts that each of us may share what he has been given. We ask this in the name of your Son, Jesus Christ, who was your most gracious gift to humankind. Amen.

21

And when you pray, you must not be like the hypocrites; for they love to stand and pray in the synagogues and at the street corners, that they may be seen by men. Truly, I say to you, they have received their reward. But when you pray, go into your room and shut the door and pray to your Father who is in secret; and your Father who sees in secret will reward you.

Chapter 6:5-6

As in giving, so in prayer. It is not the outward ceremony that accompanies public prayer that is important. True prayer takes place in the heart. It is not always easy when taking part in public worship to bear this in mind, but the fact is that if nothing is happening to our thoughts and emotions, then the act of worship must be a rather limited one.

Jesus is not condemning public prayer as such, but rather the wrong motive that some people might have. If the true motive of the one praying is to be seen by people as a "holy" person, then the prayer relationship is invalid. People may have various motives for attending church, but ultimately it is the direct personal relationship with God, in the context of the Christian community, which is of real importance.

This saying leads us to ponder on the nature of prayer. Jesus seems to be suggesting that solitary prayer is more likely to lead to a real relationship with the Father than public prayer. Of course, if a private prayer is accompanied by hypocritical posturing of any kind, that prayer might also be devalued. For example, if we try to face God with some sort of pretence in our words or thoughts, our false front is immediately spotted by him, if not by ourselves. All barriers must come down before God's holiness and love.

A good example of a person who brought all his

troubles to God without any pretence is the prophet Jeremiah. He actually felt that God had deceived him. In his despair, the prophet cursed the day of his birth, cursed his enemies and questioned God about the persecution he was subjected to by his fellow Jews. Jeremiah held nothing back. His thoughts came pouring out without any inhibition. His was a real, living relationship with the Father, forged in the suffering that is sometimes the lot of God's servants. Out of his suffering came a new understanding of God's true nature. It was only later in his life, when the situation had changed, that his private prayers or confessions were published (usually taken to be Jeremiah 11:18-23; 12:1-6; 15:10-21; 17:14-18; 18:18-23; 20:7-12 and 20:14-18).

It is easy to say with the wisdom of hindsight that Jeremiah was somewhat vindictive, but we must remember that he lived six hundred years before Jesus. What we can learn from the prophet is the sincerity and absolute honesty that should be part of private prayer. We can talk to God about any of our troubles or concerns. He knows about them anyway. Of course, prayer is much more than a confessional or a symbolic psychiatrist's couch. Worship, love and thanksgiving are all part of the prayer relationship. Sometimes a key word can help us to remember some of the aspects of prayer. One that the present writer has found helpful is the word LIGHT.

L will help us to remember the **love** of God for us and the love we should return to God.

I will help us to remember the **intercession** that Jesus makes for us and the intercession we should make for others.

G will help us to remember the **guidance** we can ask for in all that we think or speak or do.

H will help us to remember the **holiness** of God which is inseparable from his love.

T will help us to remember to give **thanks** for all the blessings we have received from God.

The word LIGHT itself is symbolic of the prayer relationship and indicates that in our prayers we are approaching the Father through the true light of the world, Jesus Christ, the Son of God. At the same time, it is the Holy Spirit who enables us to relate to the Father and the Son. God is a Trinity of persons who are One. From that ONE shines a glorious light which illuminates each one of us. When we pray we move consciously into that light and in our prayers we are given sufficient light and grace to make our way on our pilgrimage through this life, whatever happens to us.

Bible readings

Psalm 4; Luke 18:9-14; James 5:13-18.

Prayer

We ask, O Lord, when we pray, that you will guide our words and thoughts that we may worship you in truth and holiness and love. Give us the grace to pray for others and their needs before we think of our own needs. As we pray, we seek your forgiveness for the things we have done wrong each day. We also give you thanks for all the gifts you have so richly bestowed upon us and we pray that the gift of your Holy Spirit may remain with us always. Guide us in all our actions and shine your lantern on the pilgrim road that lies before us. Grant that each day we may never be far from you and that each night you may watch over our sleeping. We ask these things in the name of your Son, Jesus Christ, our Lord. Amen.

22

And in praying do not heap up empty phrases as the Gentiles do; for they think that they will be heard for their many words. Do not be like them, for your Father knows what you need before you ask him.

Chapter 6:7-8

The Greek verb used for "heaping up empty phrases" is not used elsewhere in the New Testament. It can mean "stammer" which might imply prayer without any real confidence in a response. However, Jesus goes on to condemn the use of "many words", so taken together the whole phrase seems to refer to prayer which consists of inadequate and meaningless repetition.

What Jesus would have said about the use of a "mantra" by some Christians today cannot be known. This is a technique borrowed from Hinduism and Buddhism. A mantra is a key word, sometimes believed to embody God's presence, which is repeated many times in order to induce a state of readiness for deep contemplation. A Christian might take a short prayer or a phrase like "Jesus is King" as a mantra. He could then repeat this a number of times at the beginning of a prayer session. In other words, repetition can sometimes have a positive purpose.

However, there is no doubt that repetition can also be negative. It is possible to say even the Lord's Prayer without thinking about the meaning of the words. In fact, one could go through a whole church service, repeating prayers, hymns and psalms, without really considering the meaning. This is an obvious danger for all of us, if we go to church regularly.

In referring to the Gentiles Jesus could have meant that a person could pray to one of the Roman gods a hundred times a day without any hope of a reply, for the obvious reason that such gods have no reality. In Hebrew tradition, the God Yahweh (or Jehovah) was a God of action, one whose presence was felt in every day life. The Hebrews did not philosophise about the possibility of God's existence. They knew of God's existence because of his saving grace. In their history they always looked back on the Exodus from Egypt as the prime example of God's intervention in history. Many of the psalms reflect this belief in an active God. The writer of Psalm 135, for example, recalls key events in Israelite history when God had intervened to help his chosen people. Then the psalmist writes:

Thy name, O Lord, endures for ever,
thy renown, O Lord, throughout all ages.
For the Lord will vindicate his people,
and have compassion on his servants (vv. 13-14).

It is probable that in this part of the Sermon Jesus was again criticizing the Pharisees because of their love of repeating prayers. Any Pharisee listening to Jesus's teaching on this point would have been furious at being compared to a Gentile. Jesus had this knack of hitting the nail on the head with unerring accuracy. True prayer is in the heart and presumably if we say something once in prayer God has heard our petition. Nevertheless, we do like to keep people on our prayer lists for as long as we feel they are in need of God's help. Perhaps we shall be forgiven that kind of repetition. Then again, certain favourite prayers can give great comfort when repeated thoughtfully a number of times. Take, for example, this verse from Isaiah which is often used as a prayer:

...they who wait for the Lord shall renew their strength,
they shall mount up with wings like eagles,
they shall run and not be weary,
they shall walk and not faint (Isaiah 40:31).

Direct knowledge by God of our every need is assumed in Jesus's next statement. The Father knows our requirements even before we ask him. From our limited perspective this does not always appear to be true. We sometimes doubt God's providential care because he hasn't responded to our prayers in the way that we think would be appropriate. Time and again we meet this element of mystery in our faith. There are problems which we cannot solve in this life. Job found his faith challenged by all the disasters that happened to him. In the end he found that the only response he could make was to put his trust in God, in spite of everything. God's perspective is infinite and eternal. Our perspective is limited by space and time.

Bible readings

Psalm 84; 2 Corinthians 1:12-14; 2 Peter 1:1-11.

Prayer

O God our Father, grant that the words of our prayers may be thoughtfully spoken in your presence. Help us to trust in your eternal vigilance and deliver us from all hypocrisy and shallowness, not only in our prayers, but also in our dealings with other people. Fill our hearts with love and complete our actions with your love, for the sake of Jesus Christ, your Son, our Lord. Amen.

23

Pray then like this: Our Father who art in heaven, hallowed be thy name.

Chapter 6:9

The Lord's Prayer is the best known prayer in the world. It has an immense depth of thought within its ten brief statements and petitions. We repeat the prayer so frequently that it can, if we are not careful, become a matter of habit with too little attention to the meaning of the words. Perhaps sometimes we should try to think about each part of the prayer separately, just to remind ourselves of its deeper implications. This could be extended to using each petition as a heading. So, after saying one phrase, an even longer pause for reflection could be made to allow for the verbalising of connected prayers. For example, the phrase, "Hallowed be thy name," could be followed by prayers for a deeper understanding of God's holiness and the various names we know for God, before going on to the next petition. In other words, a prayer session of some length could be based on the Lord's Prayer.

It is significant that Jesus addressed the prayer to the Father and invited his followers to do the same. This makes the prayer a family prayer and by saying it we become part of the Christian family of God. In the first phrase we are reminded that the God whom we are addressing exists in another dimension, even though we cannot see him or touch him. Nevertheless we can be acutely aware of his presence and we can frequently perceive the effects of his actions. To a large extent this is a matter of faith, for it is through the faith "sense" that we know of God's word and deed. Of course, God is with us and in his universe as well as being in heaven. The writer of Psalm 11 knew this very well when he wrote:

The Lord is in his holy temple,
the Lord's throne is in heaven;
his eyes behold,
his eyelids test the children of men (v. 4).

The word "hallowed" is not used very much in every
day chat, though we might sometimes read a rather hack-
neyed phrase in the press such as: "Lords cricket ground is
hallowed by the generations of great cricketers who have
walked across the glorious turf." When the word is applied
to God it should bring to our thoughts the idea of a being so
righteous, majestic and awesome that our imaginations
cannot encompass any limits to his power. Even his name
should be spoken with reverence, so holy is its association.

Of course, Moses had a similar thought when he was
inspired to write the third commandment. God's name
should not be taken in vain, nor be used lightly. There are
many names for God in the Bible. For example, we sometimes address him as the Almighty, or as Creator, or as
Redeemer. The word "God" is used as a form of address
but it is not as personal as the word "Father". The revealed
nature of God as personal in at least three senses gives the
Christian a wonderful insight into the divine character.
Each member of the Trinity is associated with particular
aspects of God, but we should never forget that God is One.
For example, the Father is associated with creation; the
Son with redemption; and the Holy Spirit with comforting
and guidance. If we are to hallow God's name we need to
respect every name by which he is known within the Christian faith.

God's names are often used lightly by a variety of
people. Expressions like, "Good Lord!" or "Christ Almighty!" are thrown about carelessly in daily conversation.
Most Christians would surely attempt to avoid such a misuse of holy names. Perhaps somebody needs to promote
more harmless ways of expressing surprise or annoyance.
Jewish people in ancient times were so conscious of the
danger of the misuse of God's name that they hesitated

even to pronounce it. When they read the scriptures they used the Hebrew word for "Lord", rather than Yahweh (or Jehovah). Eventually they hesitated to use even the substitute and started referring to God as "the Name". Most people would think such a practice to be extreme. It is surely right within our faith to speak to God by his name in the context of prayer or worship.

However, there are dangers in using God's name which could be more serious. We could, for example, make a promise in God's name and then break that promise (see Matthew 5:33-37). Even more serious could be the regular assent to certain principles associated with God's name, if we did not in fact try to live up to those principles. For example, we could go to church every Sunday and then behave badly during the week. Our behaviour should ideally conform with the Christian principles to which we are supposedly committed in God's name. Of course, we are all subject to various temptations and we are not perfect. But in response to God's forgiveness we can always start again. It is to be hoped that there are very few, if any, Christians who deliberately and regularly break the laws of Christian love when they have ostensibly committed themselves to a Christly way of life.

Bible readings

Genesis 28:10-17; Psalm 8; Romans 1:1-7.

Prayer

O God, we praise your holy name with all our being. We give thanks to you for the glorious revelation of the Trinity, for the Fatherhood you have shown to us, for the Incarnation of your Son and for the manifestation of your Holy Spirit. We worship you with heart and soul, O God, Father, Son, and Holy Spirit, and we ask that we may receive the blessing of your love, this day and always. Amen.

24

Thy kingdom come, Thy will be done, on earth as it is in heaven.

Chapter 6:10

The kingdom and God's will can be regarded as separate ideas, though in this saying Jesus brackets the two ideas together, to make the point that the coming of the kingdom is God's will. If it is God's will then, of course, nothing will be able to stop it from coming. It is interesting that the angel Gabriel told Mary that her son's kingdom would have no end (Luke 1:33). This suggests that God's kingdom will be both eternal and universal.

The New Testament describes the kingdom of God both as a future state and as an already existing state. The Sermon here suggests that God's kingdom is not yet completely present. Several sayings of Jesus support the notion of a future kingdom:

Truly, I say to you, there are some standing here who will not taste death before they see that the kingdom of God has come with power (Mark 9:1).

And also:

Truly, truly, I say to you, unless one is born anew, he cannot see the kingdom of God (John 3:3).

There seems to be little difference between the kingdom of heaven and the kingdom of God in New Testament usage, though Matthew seems to prefer the phrase "kingdom of heaven".

The idea that the kingdom is already here is plainly expressed:

Being asked by the Pharisees when the kingdom of God was coming, he answered them, 'The kingdom of God is not coming with signs to be observed; nor will they say, "Lo, here it is!" or "There!" for behold the kingdom of God is in the midst of you' (Luke 17:20-21).

And also:

From the days of John the Baptist until now the kingdom of heaven has suffered violence, and men of violence take it by force (Matthew 11:12).

It seems then, that the kingdom of heaven, while existing in perfect form in another dimension, also crosses over into this world. It is also developing and growing so that there is no real contradiction between saying that the kingdom is here and the kingdom is still to come. In the Lord's Prayer we are asked to pray for the full growth of the kingdom upon earth. In practical everyday terms this may mean that one day every single person on earth will recognize Christ as Saviour. It may alternatively mean that the recognition of God becomes universal, though not necessarily only through Christianity. Along with either of these interpretations no doubt the meaning encompasses the idea that all human beings will be striving to be good people and to do good actions.

Of course, the Bible does give one or two hints about the nature of the kingdom. The Old Testament, for example, talks about an age when... "They shall not hurt or destroy in all my holy mountain; for the earth shall be full of the knowledge of the Lord as the waters cover the sea" (Isaiah 11:9).

In the New Testament Jesus tells various parables about the kingdom. Elsewhere in Matthew Jesus is recorded as saying, for example, "The kingdom of heaven is like leaven which a woman took and hid in three measures of flour, till it was all leavened" (Matthew 13:33). This seems to suggest that the kingdom will grow until it is universal upon earth, as in heaven.

God's will is undoubtedly to bring the kingdom to its full growth, but it seems to need time for people to grow into it, and this can be a painful process. However, when we ask for God's will to be done here on earth, we are also asking that our human actions conform to God's will. Moreover, if we are living in the kingdom it will be our aim to bring about God's will, insofar as it lies within our power. This means starting from where we are and with the people around us. Each of us is a direct agent for bringing about God's kingdom.

Bible readings

Psalm 145; Luke 13:18-21; Matthew 25:31-46.

Prayer

O Father, grant to us entry into your kingdom so that we may live in your presence daily. May we grow in knowledge of the nature of your kingdom so that we may one day become worthy citizens of the heavenly city. And may we so live that we strive to bring about the growth of your kingdom into the hearts of all people, everywhere. Help us also to have wisdom to know your will for us, and give to us the power of mind and spirit to fulfil it. In the name of Jesus Christ, our Lord. Amen.

25

Give us this day our daily bread.

Chapter 6:11

This petition in the prayer sounds very simple and straightforward, though the English translation actually conceals a problem of interpretation in the Greek text.* However, the request for bread is clear and this refers to our regular need for food and drink. The main biblical versions agree upon this. Often we take too readily for granted the provision of our daily bread. Those who live in countries where famine rarely, if ever, occurs may be tempted to believe that they will never be hungry. Yet, our daily bread depends on good harvests, a plentiful supply of fish in the oceans and the continuing survival of other creatures that come regularly to our tables. Unless we take care of the system that God has provided it could at some time in the future break down. The ecologists and the various "Green" movements do have a contribution to make.

At the same time God's care of his creation is ongoing. While he has given us the responsibility of looking after the planet on which we live (see Genesis 1:28-30) the whole system would certainly break down if God took away his hand. It is an illusion to think that we are in complete control. Only God has the ultimate power to provide what we need. In that overall sense we do need to give thanks for all the things which he has provided. In this connection the harvest festivals of the Church express the thanks of the community for our daily bread, and often these acts of worship are very beautiful. It is also good that the concept of sharing God's gifts with others is usually part of most harvest festivals.

---

* The problem centres on the meaning of the Greek word *epioúsios* which does not appear elsewhere in biblical or classical Greek.

In addition to the need for food, each family and each individual have a series of daily needs which are specific to them. Our society basically provides each of us with food and other things in exchange for money. A person's situation can change radically if, for example, he is made redundant. In many countries there is a level below which no one theoretically is allowed to fall, but in some countries the weak or the destitute are allowed to perish. If we are fortunate enough to have jobs and a reasonable share of worldly goods we ought to be very thankful. But we ought to be conscious of the plight of those who are not so provided. Perhaps each of us ought to consider more seriously what we might do about the problem.

The Hebrew tribes under Moses were very conscious of their need for daily bread. The Bible records their thankfulness at finding manna in the desert (Exodus 16:14) and quails (Exodus 16:13). They were also able to find water when they were thirsty (Exodus 17:6). They saw the hand of God in these events. In fact, all can be explained by Moses' knowledge of the ways of the desert, acquired when he was an outlaw, and all are explicable in natural terms. The manna was probably a sticky, sweet substance found on tamarisk bushes. The quails would be migrating birds which had flopped to the ground after crossing the sea. The water would be obtained from a kind of limestone which stores water behind a thin wall, easily broken with a strong stick. Nevertheless, despite these explanations, the true reality was that the needs of the Israelites were supplied by God's providential care. Moses had spent years in the desert as an outlaw and was thus prepared for his vocation to lead his people in that inhospitable area. God does not waste our experiences, but often uses them later.

There is also a spiritual parallel to the idea of seeking our daily bread. Just as we have the physical need for sustenance, so we have a spiritual need. Many Christians would see one aspect of this need as being satisfied by the bread and wine of the communion meal. In that context the parallel between daily bread and ordinary wine, on the one hand, and spiritual food on the other hand, is obvious, whichever interpretation of the Eucharist we take. Interestingly enough, the word "eucharist" comes from a Greek word meaning "to give thanks".

Our spiritual needs and our physical needs are closely related in everyday life. The Lord's Prayer indicates that this so by including this request to God to provide our daily bread. It is placed alongside a request for forgiveness of our sins and alongside deep expressions of worship. Too often we tend to try to separate the secular from the sacred, though actually they are often so interwoven in our experience that they cannot be divided. The human being, body and soul, is one being, not two separate beings. God is with us in the work place or on the sports field, just as much as he is with us in church.

Bible readings

Psalm 145:13-21; John 6:30-35; 1 Corinthians 10:16-17.

Prayer

O Father, give us thankful hearts for your providential care. We pray that you will continue to provide for our physical needs and that the harvests of the world will be more equally shared. We also pray for our spiritual needs and ask that you will give us the bread of life, through the intercession of your Son, Jesus Christ. In his name we dare to pray, in the sure knowledge that his promises to us are for ever true. Amen.

26

And forgive us our debts, as we also have forgiven our debtors.

Chapter 6:12

In this petition we are reminded of the forgiveness that we receive from God through the intercession of the Son. The doctrine of the atonement has always been central in Christian thinking. Jesus stands beside us at the bar of God's judgement, not only on the Day of Judgement, but also each day as we say our prayers and ask forgiveness for our sins. Through his act of reconciliation on the cross and the atoning effect of this act for all humankind in all ages, we are forgiven. Consciousness of God's grace in this and many other respects should make us think deeply about any grudges against others we might be bearing in our hearts. Jesus advises us that we should find in ourselves forgiveness and love for others.

Luke's version of the Lord's prayer reads "forgive us our sins", using a different Greek word. Presumably, when Jesus taught the prayer to his disciples, probably in Aramaic, he did not have two versions. This illustrates one of the difficulties of translating from a translation. Indeed, the version of the whole prayer given by Luke seems to be based on a different interpretation of Jesus's original words. However, the second part of the statement in both Gospels does refer to forgiving those who are indebted to us. This is using terminology from every day life in a metaphorical way. Jesus uses the same symbolism in some of his parables. A good illustration of this is the parable of the servant who was released from a debt but did not release a fellow servant from a comparatively small debt (Matthew 18:23-35).

Similar thinking occurs in the terminology of redemption. A slave was redeemed or set free by a payment. The Israelites of old saw themselves as having been redeemed by God from their slavery in Egypt. This idea became spiritualized and came to refer to God's redemption of people from the slavery of sin, which means that he has paid the ransom price. A wonderful verse in the Book of Isaiah expresses this idea very well:

I have swept away your transgressions like a cloud,
and your sins are like mist;
return to me, for I have redeemed you (Isaiah 44:22).

With brilliant perception St Paul expresses the New Testament development of this idea:

God sent forth his Son, born of woman, born under the law, to redeem those who were under the law, so that we might receive adoption as sons (Galatians 4:4-5).

It is not easy to forgive people who have hurt us. But then God did not find it an easy process to forgive us for all the hurt we have caused him and other people. The atonement of the cross, as already mentioned, was a very painful process indeed. If we are to learn to forgive we must take up our crosses and follow in the footsteps of Jesus. If we offer ourselves to God in this process we shall certainly receive help. Of course, forgiving someone, or turning the other cheek, can have an amazing effect on the person so forgiven. The writer of the Book of Proverbs wrote:

If your enemy is hungry, give him bread to eat;
and if he is thirsty, give him water to drink;
for you will heap coals of fire on his head,
and the Lord will reward you (Proverbs 25:21-22).

Likewise, if we are fully aware of how forbearing God has been with us, we shall then understand the "amazing grace" which he has shown. Those who have been forgiven much will be more likely to love God and at the same time forgive others than those who have little consciousness of being forgiven. Furthermore, the capacity to absorb aggro into love in a situation of conflict often defuses the quarrel. In other words, reconciliation can then take place. This is precisely what Christ did. He absorbed all the aggro in history into his love.

Bible readings

Psalm 103; Luke 7:36-50; Ephesians 4:25-32.

Prayer

O Father, we know that you have forgiven us so many transgressions against yourself and others. Give us the grace to learn to forgive, as we are forgiven. Take away from our hearts all bitterness and hate and fill the whole of our being with your love. Show us how to love others as we walk along life's pathways, that we may follow in the footsteps of your Son, Jesus Christ, our Lord. Amen.

27

**And lead us not into temptation,
but deliver us from evil.**

Chapter 6:13

This petition has always been difficult to interpret because at first sight it seems to suggest that God is deliberately going to put temptation in our way. However, the Greek word translated "temptation" often means "test" or "trial". This is fairly widely known and "put us not to the test" is usually accepted as a reasonable interpretation of the phrase. The second part of the petition supports this idea of a spiritual test. Of course, Jesus himself went through a spiritual trial in his temptation and we do often speak of people being tested in terms of vocation, for example. Perhaps the petition implies a request that we should not be tested beyond our capacity.

Sometimes we do find ourselves in a very testing position. We may have a difficult decision to make. We may indeed be tempted to do something that is against our better judgement. King David, for example, allowed himself to be drawn into an affair with Bathsheba when he knew that it was wrong, because she was already married. He allowed himself to be further drawn into an already difficult situation by deliberately arranging for Bathsheba's husband, Uriah, to be killed in battle (see 2 Samuel 11). Thankfully, not many people are tempted to go as far as that, though like David we are all subject to human weakness. The well known saying, "There but for the grace of God go I", is surely applicable to all of us, though why some people seem to be tested more than others is something of a mystery.

The account of Jesus's temptation in the wilderness, which must have been recounted by Jesus himself to his disciples, shows that various options were open to him.

What kind of Messiah was he going to be? How could he demonstrate that he was the Messiah? (see Matthew 4:1-11). The agent of the temptation is portrayed as Satan and, indeed, the Lord's Prayer asks for deliverance from "evil" and this can be interpreted as deliverance from Satan. Some people believe that Satan is an actual person. Others believe that he is a symbolic personification of evil. Whichever view is taken there is little doubt of the reality of evil as a force in the world. Those who remember the Holocaust of the Jewish people during the Second World War or the injustice of apartheid in South Africa should be in little doubt about that.

Yet, an even more potent force in the world is the saving power of God. The ancient Israelites were fully aware of this because they experienced God's deliverance in very practical ways. As explained in a previous section, the most memorable event in their history was the Exodus. They interpreted this event as an act of deliverance by God himself. Moses acted as the intermediary, but God's power was revealed in many signs and wonders, not least in the crossing of the Reed Sea (or Red Sea) (see Exodus 13-14). Such signs and wonders are often explained away as natural phenomena. In fact, the nine plagues can be explained in this way, except perhaps for the selective deaths of the Egyptian first born. Even in that case the deaths could have been caused by a natural disease (see Exodus 5-12).

But God often works through nature and through people, using existing structures. Suppose, for example, a Christian and an atheist were watching the Red Sea crossing. The Christian might say, "What a wonderful example of God's providence!" The atheist, on the other hand might comment, "My, weren't they lucky!" The miraculous part in a saving event may be the timing. This is not to deny the possibility of the supernatural, because many people in the Bible and in the history of the Christian faith have testified that miracles have occurred. Indeed, what greater miracle could there be than the resurrection? The biblical miracle stories are familiar to most Christians; and in the modern age also healing miracles in particular are well documented, as at the shrine of Lourdes.

From the very fact of the resurrection and the saving power which accompanied it, we can be certain that God has the power to deliver us from evil. When Jesus was crucified he was taking part in a cosmic struggle between good and evil; and defeated the power of evil and conquered death in the sense that he showed death to be a positive change from one state to another state of being. Death is not an end, but a beginning. With that central fact of the faith in mind we can arm ourselves through prayer against the powers of Satan. As St Paul wrote,

> Put on the whole armour of God, that you may be able to stand against the wiles of the devil (Ephesians 6:11).

Bible readings

Psalm 37:1-11; Romans 7:18-25; 2 Thessalonians 3:1-5.

Prayer

O Father, as Jesus Chist your Son was tempted and was strengthened in prayer and grace, so may we receive strength in times of trial. We pray that your Holy Spirit may watch over us and that the wiles of Satan may always be frustrated. Save us, O Lord, when we are in danger and deliver us from all evil. We ask these things in the name of that same Jesus Christ, who conquered sin and death, once and for all time. Amen.

28

**For if you forgive men their trespasses, your heavenly
Father also will forgive you; but if you do not forgive men
their trespasses, neither will your Father forgive your
trespasses.**

Chapter 6:14-15

This saying is an expansion of the petition in the
Lord's Prayer in verse 12. That such a statement
immediately follows illustrates the importance of
forgiveness in the Christian life. Jesus said quite a lot about
this subject. The parable of the Prodigal Son is a good
example (see also the comments on Matthew 5:7). We all
know this story so well and we all identify with the son
who is forgiven when he returns to his father. God's forgiveness is always there when we return or repent and
come back to him. Sometimes, though, our part may be that
of the son who stayed at home. In such a case we have to
try to understand the positions of other people in difficult
situations (see Luke 15:11-32). The ability to sympathise,
or better still to empathise, with others, is helpful to our
own development. As somebody once said, "If you wish to
criticise someone wear that person's moccasins for six
months."

An interesting aspect of this saying in the Sermon is the
logical equivalence of our forgiveness of others with God's
forgiveness of us. The one seems to depend on the other. At
first sight this would appear to be in accord with the rules
of natural justice. If we are not prepared to forgive those
who have offended us why should God forgive us when we
have offended him? However, we cannot really attribute
such small mindedness to Almighty God. He is surely
above this kind of tit for tat approach. What may lie behind
the statement is the idea that, if we are holding things
against other people, we ourselves are not in the kind of

mental state in which we can receive forgiveness from God. If a person is bearing a grudge and won't let it go, there is little room for the love of God, because the heart is full of hate.

To receive God's forgiveness we surely need to be fully aware of our own shortcomings. If we have not brought everything in our lives to him, if there is a part of us which is holding back, if we are not fully open to the divine love, then there is a barrier which prevents us from being forgiven.

Another deeply relevant point is that we also have to learn to forgive ourselves. This does not mean that we can lightly throw aside any hurt we have done to others, whether it was done intentionally or unintentionally. We need to make what amends we can. This may mean trying to reconcile differences with the other person we know we have hurt. We need to take the hurt to our own hearts to realize fully what the person we have hurt may feel like. At the same time, there must come a point when we have to accept God's forgiveness. To hoard guilt may be just as much a barrier against God's love as not to feel guilty at all. Each situation is different. Only in a prayer relationship can we be aware of the right time to put aside old guilt. One factor that may be necessary before we can do this is the acceptance of the full burden of the hurt we may have caused another upon ourselves, and then to allow Christ to take the burden from us. As Jesus also said:

Come to me, all who labour and are heavy laden, and
I will give you rest (Matthew 11:28).

Personal relationships can have their difficulties, even within marriage. Husband and wife may hurt each other and feel the need to be reconciled. Similarly, parent and child or brother and sister may for various reasons be involved in hurtful situations. Often, these are resolved and the family bond grows stronger. Likewise, close friends may sometimes differ, come together again, and feel afterwards that they are even closer than they were before. It is when the process of reconciliation does not take place that sad developments may occur. Pride is often a barrier. It is always a great pity when loving relationships come to an end. If one person can find the strength in humility to offer forgiveness and reconciliation this can often heal the breach. For Christians the way forward should be clear, though not necessarily easy:

> ...do not let the sun go down on your anger, and give no opportunity to the devil (Ephesians 4:26-27).

Bible readings

Psalm 25:11-18; Matthew 18:21-22; Romans 3:21-26.

Prayer

O Father, dwell within us and fill our hearts with your love. Give us the grace to know when we are forgiven and at the same time give us the will to forgive others as you forgive us. Remove all barriers that are raised by pride and self will so that your love can flow freely through our lives and touch all those who are around us. Amen.

29

And when you fast, do not look dismal, like the hypo-crites, for they disfigure their faces that their fasting may be seen by men. Truly, I say to you, they have received their reward. But when you fast, anoint your head and wash your face, that your fasting may not be seen by men but by your Father who is in secret; and your Father who is in secret will reward you.

Chapter 6:16-18

This saying is similar to previous ones in suggesting that the spiritual life is essentially a private matter and one's prayerful activities should not be paraded in public, especially if publicity should be the objective. In the time of Jesus, wearing sackcloth and ashes often ac-companied fasting and it would then be obvious to every-one that a fast was being followed. However, Jesus recommends that the face should be washed and the head anointed so that the discipline would be known only to God. Anointing was usually associated with joyous occa-sions. Some members of the Church do, of course, smear the face with ashes on Ash Wednesday, for the first day of the Lenten fast. This practice is to honour Jesus, not only by symbolically imitating his forty-day fast, but also by using a sort of sacramental commitment to start any discipline they may have undertaken. During the rest of Lent they can presumably follow the advice given in the Sermon.

While Jesus was fasting and meditating in the desert, one of his temptations was to end his fast by turning stones into bread. The purpose of the fast is not made explicit in the Bible story, but it seems partly, at any rate, to have been a testing discipline undertaken in order to explore the na-ture of his vocation as Son of God. Christians vary greatly in their view of fasting. Whatever position we hold our-selves it is surely wise to respect the practice of others.

In Old Testament times fasts were sometimes proclaimed in times of national emergency, in which case everyone would be known to be fasting simultaneously (see, for example, Ezra 8:21-23). Individuals undertook fasts for various reasons. Fasting could accompany prayer for a sick person (see Psalm 35:13-14). When King Ahab was penitent he fasted in order to show the seriousness of his change of heart (see 1 Kings 21:27-29). David and his companions fasted when they mourned for Saul and Jonathan (see 2 Samuel 1:11-12).

It is interesting that John the Baptist encouraged his followers to fast whereas Jesus appears to have been less rigorous in this respect at least, though obviously the demands of Jesus were very rigorous in other directions. In any case, it is surely more demanding to fast secretly while outwardly putting on a cheerful face, than it is to fast openly. When Jesus was challenged about his attitude on this matter he said:

Can the wedding guests mourn as long as the bridegroom is with them? (Matthew 9:15).

He then told the parables about the new wine bursting old bottles and the patch of unshrunk material tearing away from an old garment. This shows that he was consciously breaking away from traditions which had become outworn. In modern times we may occasionally have to do the same. Customs of a past generation are not always appropriate for the present generation. At the same time we have to distinguish between what needs to be changed and what it would be inadvisable to change. For example, it might be good to hold the sacrament of Baptism in front of the congregation at a major church service, instead of at a private service, but it would be inadvisable to change the intrinsic nature of the sacrament because it is so central to the Christian faith.

In general terms, whatever kind of discipline the Christian undertakes, it can, if properly planned, undergird the events of his/her daily life and strengthen the resolve in difficult circumstances. To do this cheerfully and without ostentation may be even more effective. To have a spiritual powerhouse working away within us, as is surely the case when we commit ourselves seriously to Christ, is not only helpful to ourselves, but can enable us to give others encouragement along some of life's thornier pathways.

The disciplines of Lent seem to be less used than previously. Perhaps people cannot always perceive the positive purpose of such a discipline. However, it may be that a positive discipline is of more value than a negative discipline. To do some extra reading and prayers every day and to attend group meetings and extra church services might be considered by some people as more appropriate than denying oneself of things to eat. To be sure, denial can be made positive by contributing any money saved to a charity. It is difficult to lay down rules in this area. So often the right discipline for an individual is a matter of temperament. In any case, one invitation by Jesus is unequivocal:

> If any man would come after me, let him deny himself and take up his cross and follow me (Matthew 16:24).

Bible readings

Joel 2:12-14; 2 Corinthians 11:16-29; Acts 13:1-3.

Prayer

O God, when we seek to fast or pray, give us the strength to hold to our discipline and grant that our characters may be formed in imitation of your Son, Jesus Christ. Show us how to be cheerful and happy each day at the same time as we discipline ourselves each day, that we may help others as you have helped us. We ask that your Holy Spirit may so guide us in our words, thoughts and actions, that we may prove ourselves acceptable as citizens of your heavenly kingdom. Amen.

30

Do not lay up for yourselves treasures on earth, where moth and rust consume and where thieves break in and steal, but lay up for yourselves treasure in heaven, where neither moth nor rust consumes and where thieves do not break in and steal. For where your treasure is, there will your heart be also.

Chapter 6:19-21

In any interpretation of this saying it is manifestly true that anything we value on earth has no permanence. The intention of the text is not necessarily to refer to money and worldly goods, though these are surely included. The wider meaning implies that whatever we place at the forefront of our lives will come to an end, unless it is undergirded by ultimate values. Our "consuming" interests may include football or philately, films or fishing, and these are positive and good things; but they are only on loan to us, just as our whole lives are on loan from God. So what are the ultimate values? What does it mean to say that we should place our treasure in heaven?

Another way of putting this would be to ask what we can take to heaven with us if we eventually go there. It is fairly obvious that we cannot take our houses, our bank balances, our pictures, our books, our gardens, or our golf clubs. What we can take is what makes up our personalities, our characters, our mental awareness, or if you like, our souls. What memories we keep we do not know. What kind of life we are going to when we pass over, we do not know. What the nature of our faculties of our heavenly bodies will be, we do not know. However, it would be reasonable to surmise that the next life will be even more wonderful than this earthly life at its best.

If we accept the teaching of the Bible and the highest ideals of the Christian faith, we know that love, truth, goodness, faithfulness and awareness of beauty are some of the ultimate values that exist in our lives. We know that we ought to love God with all our hearts and our neighbour as ourselves. In some sense that we cannot fully understand with our present limited knowledge, these are God's heavenly treasures. If we value these things above all earthly things we shall have something of value to take with us to the next stage of our development.

Of course, this does not mean that our worldly interests and possessions are completely valueless. But if we have a beautiful house which is not filled with love, then it is an empty house. If we have a bank balance which is used only for selfish purposes, then it is going to end in spiritual bankruptcy. If all the things we enjoy doing are not ultimately related to a spiritual interpretation of life, then these things will be like the cold ashes of a dead fire. The great Christian writer, Thomas à Kempis, may have had Jesus's Sermon in mind when he wrote, "So passes the glory of the world" (*Sic transit gloria mundi*).

There are many wonderful things in this life if they are properly used and shared with others. We can imagine also that there must be many more wonderful things in heaven. But if we are to be ready for the heavenly experience we must turn our thoughts to the heavenly kingdom. We can be part of the heavenly experience now. We can live in God's kingdom now. We have been invited to do so and if we refuse that invitation we are refusing the most wonderful gift that our experience can offer.

Of course, we cannot by the nature of things have our minds at high spiritual altitudes all the time. It is more a question of climbing the heavenly mountain now and again in order to look at the landscapes of God's kingdom. This is what having a prayer life is about. It is also based on the pattern of what Jesus himself did. He spent most of his ministry preaching and helping people, and sometimes going to parties, but he also had regular times for prayer. At these times he often quite literally climbed a mountain to get away from the world and to spend some time with heaven in his view.

Bible readings

Isaiah 33:5-6; John 3:31-36; 2 Peter 1:1-11.

Prayer

O Father of all and Creator of all, you have given us many treasures to look after and to enjoy. We pray that our hearts may be turned towards those treasures which are heavenly, rather than towards earthly things alone. Sanctify all that we do in this life so that we may be prepared for the life to come. We ask these things in the name of Jesus Christ, your Son. Amen.

31

The eye is the lamp of the body. So, if your eye is sound, your whole body will be full of light; but if your eye is not sound, your whole body will be full of darkness. If then the light in you is darkness, how great is the darkness!

Chapter 6:22-23

While all the senses are important, sight is certainly one of the most useful. The eye is critically important in giving light to the whole body in terms of our orientation towards the outside world. But Jesus, of course, is using the eye as a metaphor for the spirit within us, the "inward eye" mentioned by the poet Wordsworth. If the essential spirit which guides our consciousness does not give light as the eye gives light, then our whole inner being is in darkness. If our thoughts are always on the darker side of human experience, then the light of Christ has little opportunity to guide us on the true path. Yet again Jesus pierces to the heart of life's true meaning.

The Jewish rabbis believed that two spirits were at constant war within a person, a good spirit and an evil spirit. This thought is true to our experience. Very often we seem to be at war within ourselves, striving to do what is right when some impulse is dragging us in the opposite direction. For example, a man may be seriously tempted to alter some key figures in a report because they show him in a bad light, but his conscience tells him clearly that this would be wrong, so after a struggle he manages to resist the temptation.

Many religions use the symbolism of light and darkness in order to contrast the virtues of life with the vices. Perhaps the most outstanding example is Zoroastrianism, which teaches that there is constant war between the powers of light and the powers of darkness. In general, light is symbolic of truth, wisdom and love. Darkness is symbolic of chaos, folly and evil. It is not difficult to find examples of times when large parts of the world have been in danger from the powers of darkness. The Second World War is a good example. At that time evil forces tried to take over the whole world. It is important to note, though, that the evil was active in people, just as the opposing good was active in the human soul. It is also important to remember that good and evil were operative together in individuals and nations on both sides of the conflict.

At creation God said, "Let there be light," and the light was separated from the darkness. That, of course, referred to the physical world, but nevertheless God is portrayed as bringing order out of chaos. In the first chapter of John's Gospel light and darkness are contrasted in relation to the Word, the Word that was with God at the beginning of creation. But John takes the imagery into the realm of the spiritual struggle:

> The light shines in the darkness, and the darkness has not overcome it (John 1:5).

To put this in a slightly different way, Jesus was victorious in his struggle against the powers of evil, sin and death, and though the struggle continues, the ultimate victory of good over evil is assured.

Jesus is also characterized as the light of the world elsewhere in John's Gospel. John quotes Our Lord himself as saying:

> I am the light of the world; he who follows me will not walk in darkness, but will have the light of life (John 8:12).

The birth of Jesus is associated with light entering a dark world and Christmas is a festival of light for all Christians when we celebrate the guiding star seen by the Magi and the shining vision of angels seen by the shepherds. Simeon was aware of this symbolism when he spoke the *Nunc Dimittis*:

...for mine eyes have seen thy salvation which thou hast prepared in the presence of all peoples, a light for revelation to the Gentiles, and for glory to thy people Israel (Luke 2:30-32).

If we allow the light of Jesus to illuminate our lives in every way, not only in guiding our actions, but also and perhaps more importantly, in shining upon our deepest thoughts, then we can be sure that "the eye is the lamp of the body" in a very real and ultimate sense, as far as we are concerned.

Bible Readings

Psalm 27; Isaiah 9:2-7; Philippians 2:12-16.

Prayer

O Father of light, who created all light, shine upon us the light of your Spirit, that we may stand with your Son, the light of the world, in the universal light of your love; that we may be illuminated by the wisdom of your Holy Spirit burning within us. We ask you in the name of Jesus, the Lord, Amen.

32

No one can serve two masters; for either he will hate
the one and love the other, or he will be devoted to the
one and despise the other. You cannot serve God and
mammon.

Chapter 6:24

The punch line in this saying is, of course, the last
sentence. The analogy of a servant is used to emphasize the point. If the servant has two bosses he
will be confused in his loyalties. Anyone who has been
placed in that position at work will understand this very well.

The word "mammon" is really an Aramaic word and is
probably one of the few words in the New Testament
actually used by Jesus. Mammon refers to money or property. It didn't necessarily have a bad meaning. Jewish
rabbis in the early centuries of the Common Era used the
word without any judgemental association. However, it is
used in one of the parables in Luke's Gospel and is described there as "unrighteous mammon" (Luke 16:9). Yet,
in that same context, commenting on the parable of the
dishonest steward, Jesus advised people to make friends by
using mammon. This may be a recognition by Jesus that
people need to act at times according to the ways of the
world because that is the only way to influence events.
Luke then quotes the saying used by Matthew here as a
further comment following the parable (v. 13).

Jesus often made challenging statements and it is sometimes difficult to understand precisely what he meant. Was
he condemning possessions of all kinds? Certainly he didn't
possess very much himself in terms of worldly goods and
he several times advised people to give away all their
money to the poor. Some Christians have taken this advice
literally, as in the case of St Francis. On the other hand,
Jesus could have been condemning money or property

which had been gained by dishonest means. Or he could have been criticizing the love of money when it detracted from love of God.

Perhaps one of St Paul's often misquoted sayings about money clarifies the issue. He wrote:

For the love of money is the root of all evils... (1 Timothy 6:10).

Paul implies that it is not the normal use of money which is evil, but loving it too much. Jesus himself recognizes that money is necessary. For example, when challenged by the Pharisees to say whether it was lawful to pay taxes to Caesar or not, Jesus gave the famous reply:

Render therefore to Caesar the things that are Caesar's, and to God the things that are God's (Matthew 22:21).

What the Sermon does in condemning mammon is to challenge us to think about our resources and how we are using them. If our vocation is to become a monk or a nun then we would indeed, like St Francis, own very few personal possessions. On the other hand, if our Christian vocation is to marry and bring up children, then we need and ought to earn money in order to bring up our families. Yet again, we may not have family commitments and our vocation may be to work as a teacher or as a plumber, using whatever skills God has given us, in which case we would still need money in order to survive in our society.

What every Christian must do is consider his total commitments in relation to his Christian vocation and then decide what his priorities ought to be. Those who are in a position to do so may well conclude that a proportion of their money has to be used to relieve the suffering or poverty of others. It is a matter of conscience. What Jesus is saying is that we should not give greater priority to money than we do to God.

Bible readings

Psalm 10; James 2:1-8; Revelation 3:14-22.

Prayer

O Lord, we offer ourselves and all that we have to you. We know that you have created all that we are and have and that any talents we possess are gifts from you. Help us, therefore, to learn to share our gifts and our possessions with those who are deprived by human agency of their share of the world's riches. We ask this in the name of Jesus Christ, our Lord. Amen.

33

Therefore I tell you, do not be anxious about your life, what you shall eat or what you shall drink, nor about your body, what you shall put on. Is not life more than food, and the body more than clothing? Look at the birds of the air; they neither sow nor reap nor gather into barns, and yet your heavenly Father feeds them. Are you not of more value than they? And which of you by being anxious can add one cubit to his span of life? And why are you anxious about clothing? Consider the lilies of the field, how they grow; they neither toil nor spin; yet I tell you, even Solomon in all his glory was not arrayed like one of these. But if God so clothes the grass of the field, which today is alive and tomorrow is thrown into the oven, will he not much more clothe you, O men of little faith? Therefore do not be anxious, saying, "What shall we eat?" or "What shall we drink?" or "What shall we wear?" For the Gentiles seek all these things; and your heavenly Father knows that you need them all. But seek first his kingdom and his righteousness, and all these things shall be yours as well. Therefore do not be anxious about tomorrow, for tomorrow will be anxious for itself. Let the day's own trouble be sufficient for the day.

Chapter 6:25-34

L ike many of Jesus's sayings this one is about getting our priorities right. What are the really important things in life? Jesus suggests that God's kingdom and our moral attitudes should be prior to any worries we might have about our daily needs. The examples he gives of food and drink and clothing are considered by most people to be absolute necessities. Many would ask, "What sort of quality of life would we have if we did not have these essentials?" Yet again, some would say that spiritual development is not encouraged by deprivation. At one level of thinking these statements are true. But Jesus goes a step further and suggests that God the Father will provide for our daily needs if we put ourselves in his care.

The problem is compounded in modern society by the number of things we seem to regard as essential. The television, the washing machine, central heating, power supplies, refrigerators and freezers are regarded by many as necessities for a reasonable sort of life. If Jesus were alive today, however, he would no doubt say the same as he did two thousand years ago. He might use different examples, though the ones he chose are still absolute basic necessities, but he would surely still say that trust in God is the first priority.

Did Jesus mean that we shouldn't bother to work or try to produce food, drink and clothing for ourselves and others? That seems very unlikely. After all, Jesus himself worked with his hands in a necessary trade. At the same time, when his ministry began he gave up his work and asked his disciples to do the same. We know that sometimes they went hungry and had to resort to plucking ears of corn in a field (Matthew 12:1). At other times Jesus and sometimes his disciples were invited to dine with friends (Luke 11:37). They managed, above all, to survive on faith. It is perhaps not surprising that they were criticized for not formally fasting, for no doubt they had to fast often enough because of the life they were leading.

There are people today who commit themselves as completely as Jesus and his disciples to a vocation and sometimes the followers of such vocations voluntarily embrace poverty. One of the vows taken by monks and nuns is the vow of poverty. But for most people earning a living is the norm. Nevertheless, it is part of the Christian vocation, wherever it may lead, to place ourselves completely in God's hands. This is not only a matter of faith in the teachings of the Church, but it also involves trusting God in all situations. Let us face the fact that people do sometimes have unhappy experiences. They lose their jobs, they lose loved ones, they are involved in accidents, they fall ill and so on. But if we have complete trust in God then the impact of such unhappy situations is placed in a true perspective. If our faith is big enough we can face whatever experiences life has to offer. Worrying does not solve the problems, though of course endeavour sometimes does. If our creative energies are directed towards finding solutions in the context of prayer and if we leave our fears and worries in God's hands, then we are doing all we can.

Regular worship and prayer provide some of the basic ingredients for a happy life. If we try to love God and our neighbour, if we attempt to live our lives according to Christian principles and if at the same time we remember that God is a person, not an abstraction, then all other aspects of our lives will be seen in their true light. Talking things over with God, at the same time remembering his glory and his might, together with his ability to control all things, quietens the troubled soul in a miraculous way. Living for today and not dwelling too much on either the past or the future is also important. If we live each day as if it were God's gift to us, as indeed it is, then we will be able to accept the gift with joy and to use it to the full.

Bible readings

Deuteronomy 31:7-8; Psalm 65:9-13; Matthew 10:5-15.

Prayer

O Lord, give us faith and trust in your providence in the sure knowledge that all things are ultimately in your care. Teach us to bring our concerns to you in prayer and give us the wisdom to know when our efforts are needless. Yet, when we need your strength and power within us please guide and help us so that we may be able to change those things which we have the power to change. We ask this through Jesus Christ, our Lord. Amen.

34

Judge not that you be not judged. For with the judgement you pronounce you will be judged, and the measure you give will be the measure you get. Why do you see the speck that is in your brother's eye, but do not notice the log that is in your own eye? Or how can you say to your brother, "Let me take the speck out of your eye," when there is the log in your own eye? You hypocrite, first take the log out of your own eye, and then you will see clearly to take the speck out of your brother's eye.

Chapter 7:1-5.

One of the difficulties we all have is in trying to see ourselves clearly. As the poet Robert Burns wrote:

O wad some Pow'r the giftie gie us
To see oursels as others see us...

Some of our faults we can identify, but others are less easy to see. Yet, at the same time we often unerringly claim to identify other people's faults. However, as we grow in our spiritual lives we become less liable to criticize others and more likely to overlook their faults. Hopefully, we also become more skilled in identifying where we ourselves are going wrong.

Judgement is part of the Christian tradition. It is also built into our legal system. Society makes judgements and punishes people. Professional people study the law and adminster it, though the lay person also has a part in the process. If we did not have a legal system with its penalties, presumably chaos would result. So in that sense judgements are a necessary part of life. We need to distinguish from that sort of judgement the personal judgements we are tempted to make about others, often about very minor aspects of behaviour, though sometimes about more serious matters. We rarely know the full facts about other people's problems. Nor do we know the reasons for their decisions. Therefore, it is foolish to make superficial judgements.

Take, for example, the man who appears to those arround him to be bad tempered and inconsiderate. He is very unpopular at work and seems to have offended nearly everyone in the office at one time or another. The fact is he has very considerable domestic problems. One of his children is handicapped and there are financial difficulties. His wife has run away from the problems and the man is left to cope on his own. He gets very little sleep because of the handicapped child. Nobody at work knows this background and the man is condemned outright as a social misfit. One day, however, the man's problems are revealed to a colleague through a third party. The people at the office begin to show a measure of understanding. The man reacts readily to these friendly overtures and his behaviour at work improves considerably. One or two colleagues even offer practical help and the man is overwhelmed by this kindness. His outward character changes completely and he begins to show himself as a caring and considerate person.

Of course, to say that people should not be judged does not mean that the Church should condone serious sins. There may be occasions when cruelty to animals or children, for example, needs to be condemned. It is a pity that we do not know more about why people are cruel to each other. If we knew more about human motivation we could perhaps do something to help people to reform themselves. Christian love has the capacity to change people, but it cannot be imposed on someone. The love of Christ has to work within a person in order to bring about change, and that person needs to learn to cooperate with the creative process of growth which is offered to all of us. We should feel sorry for those who have not become aware of this work of the Spirit of God which is helping each one of us to develop into a child of God.

If we understand what is happening to ourselves in our

spiritual growth, we can begin to understand our own failings and then begin to have a glimmer of understanding about other people's problems. As we begin to understand we may possibly become less critical of others. Those who are always criticizing other people, especially about minor matters, have a deep-seated cause of unhappiness within themselves. Probably they are not aware of this and even more probably they do not understand what Jesus meant by his parable of the speck in another's eye and the log in our own eye. To be forgiven is to learn to forgive others. To be aware of our own faults and why we commit them, helps us to learn a little about other people's failings and their causes.

We must remember nevertheless that at no time did Jesus ever condone serious sin. He did, in fact, make some very important statements about God's judgement. Take these words, for example:

> I tell you, on the day of judgement men will render account for every careless word they utter; for by your words you will be justified, and by your words you will be condemned (Matthew 12:36-37).

Yet, while he was upon earth he sometimes forgave sinners and he sometimes deliberately showed love for sinners. His whole life's work was about saving people from sin by a process of self-giving love. When he did criticize people it was quite often for hypocrisy. He made the point strongly that if we judge other people we are in great danger of being hypocritical. We need to learn to turn our critical judgement upon ourselves.

Shakespeare may have had this saying of Jesus in mind when he wrote:

> Forbear to judge, for we are sinners all (Henry VI, Part II, III, 31)

116

Bible readings

Psalm 32; Luke 5:17-26; Romans 14:10-19.

Prayer

O Lord, please help us to see ourselves as you see us. Give us an understanding of our own faults and grant us the wisdom to understand other people's faults. We pray for forgiveness for our own sins and for the grace not to judge other people, but rather to leave them to your love and judgement. We ask these things in the name of Jesus Christ, our Lord. Amen.

35

Do not give dogs what is holy; and do not throw your pearls before swine, lest they trample them underfoot and turn to attack you.

Chapter 7:6

This saying has always been very difficult to interpret. Some have argued that Jesus was stating that the Gospel, at that stage, was intended only for Jews. Certainly in Matthew 10:5 the twelve disciples are instructed to "go nowhere among the Gentiles". Interestingly enough, the Canaanite woman (Matthew 15:21-28) was told that Jesus had only come to the lost sheep of Israel. When she knelt in front of Jesus to appeal to him to heal her daughter, Jesus replied that the children's bread should not be given to dogs. The woman would not give up and she said that even the dogs could obtain crumbs from their master's table. Jesus then relented and cured the woman's daughter.

Some early Christians interpreted the saying as referring to the Eucharist in the sense that unworthy people should not be admitted to the communion table. However, that can scarcely have been the direct meaning intended by Jesus when he was teaching. It does seem that dogs and swine were regarded as ritually unclean animals and they were not generally respected.

At 2 Peter 2:22 these animals are contrasted with the idea of holiness. The implication could be then that unholy people should be avoided because they do not respect God or his servants.

Some people have argued that, as the statement follows a very liberal saying about not judging people, it is really a counterbalance to say, "Well, yes, we shouldn't judge people, but at the same time there is a limit." What we are not sure of is the exact order in which Jesus might have given this body of teaching. It could be that Matthew has arranged the sayings and consequently he could be the one who is trying to balance one saying against another.

Whichever interpretation we care to take, there is a central idea stating a general truth which was valid in the time of Jesus and which is still valid today. Some people will not accept the ideals of the Christian faith and will attack those who try to preach the Gospel to them. Some people will despise the idea of holiness and will reject God. Some people will turn away from what is spiritually good and wholesome and deliberately seek evil. They are, of course, to be pitied and we ought to pray that God will call them back and that they will respond. The parable of the Prodigal Son is for all of us, for at some time each of us has been or will be, spiritually speaking, in the position of the spendthrift son. He ended up looking after swine, an unhappy fate for a Jewish person at that time.

Does the saying mean that we ought not to try to present the truths of the Gospel to those in our generation who do not wish to receive them? Probably not. But it surely means that we try to avoid situations where the Christian faith and the Church can be be wilfully sullied by spiritual vandals. There are possible dangers in satirical programmes on television or in scurrilous articles in the press or even in new dictionary definitions. We should hopefully try to preserve our sense of humour but at the same time we should be aware that there is a line of respect and decency which ought not to be crossed. What do we do when we feel that such a line has been crossed? This, of course, is up to the individual, though public protests sometimes seem to make matters worse. Possibly, refusing to cooperate by not watching or not reading the offending material may be the answer. The individual must decide.

Then again, church buildings are being vandalised more frequently, sometimes in very unpleasant ways. What is the poor clergy person to do? If the church is closed when not being used for a service, then some people will be deprived of the comfort of praying in church. On the other hand, if the church is left open, anything movable is likely to be stolen. The guardians of each church building have a difficult job to do in guarding the outward symbols of God's holiness. They deserve the moral and practical support of all Christians.

Bible readings

Isaiah 6:1-10; Psalm 50; Jude vv. 17-23.

Prayer

O most holy God, Father of all creation, we ask that your word and will may prevail in the world and that your servants may find strength and inspiration to preach the Gospel of Christ to all nations. May all peoples come to respect and honour your glorious majesty and holiness. We pray that in your mercy you may bring those who despise your word to an understanding of your love in the light of your Holy Spirit. Amen.

36

Ask, and it will be given you; seek, and you will find; knock, and it will be opened to you. For every one who asks receives, and he who seeks finds, and to him who knocks it will be opened. Or what man of you, if his son asks him for bread, will give him a stone? Or if he asks for a fish, will give him a serpent? If you then, who are evil, know how to give good gifts to your children, how much more will your Father who is in heaven give good things to those who ask him!

Chapter 7:7-11

In this saying Jesus emphasizes that our prayers are heard and answered and assures us that, in any case, God is watching over our needs and will give us what is appropriate. The idea that God always listens to prayers is difficult for some people, especially those who are beginning to pray. The problem of apparently unanswered prayer then arises. However, Jesus's comparison with the human father is useful in understanding this problem. A father will give his child what is good for him and this is not necessarily the same as what the child wants. Sometimes a father has to say, "No", or, " Wait and see", or, "Not just yet", or, "That is bad for you."

Nevertheless, it is very hard when a loved one is seriously ill or in some kind of danger and our prayers for his or her recovery or safety seem to be ignored. Some people have found it helpful in such circumstances to use the idea of long term spiritual development which continues into the next life. What seems to us to be a tragedy ending in death may, in fact, be indicative of a step upwards on the spiritual ladder. This could be true for the person we have lost but it could also be true for those who are left behind. Difficulties have to be faced and overcome and in the process we can develop as people, becoming stronger and more committed in the faith. Of course, if we turn away from God then we may stop growing for a time.

However, Jesus himself was put to the test and had to accept extreme hardship which took him through the barrier of death. When he was praying in Gethsemane he said, "My Father, if it be possible, let this cup pass from me; nevertheless, not as I will, but as thou wilt" (Matthew 26:39). Then, on the cross he gave a cry of dereliction saying, "My God, my God, why hast thou forsaken me?" (Matthew 27:46). Of course, it is well known that these words are a quotation from Psalm 22, which actually ends in the triumph of the sufferer. Even so, these two quotations show that Jesus accepted the ultimate in human suffering and yet knew that it was God's will. Therefore, we should be able to understand the saying in the Sermon in the light of Jesus's own experience. The message is that the Father is caring for us, however difficult the circumstances seem at any one time.

Jesus promises that the Father will "give good things to those who ask him". In creating us, the Father has already given us wonderful gifts: our bodies and minds, our five senses, a beautiful world to live in, people and animals to love and care for, thousands of interesting things to do. We can be assured that greater gifts are to come, despite any hardships we may be going through at a particular time. When life is at its best in this world it is good indeed. What life must be like in the next world can only be imagined as an experience even more wonderful. But we do have to be ready for that experience. If we lead selfish lives and ignore the advice that the Bible gives us, then we shall not be prepared for the life to come. As Francis Thompson put it in his famous poem "The Hound of Heaven":

...Tis ye, 'tis your estranged faces,
That miss the many splendoured thing.

Bible readings

Psalm 62; Luke 18:1-8; John 14:1-14.

Prayer

O Father, when we pray and ask for your help we know that you are listening to our prayers. We ask for the grace to wait for your response to the needs of those for whom we are praying and the wisdom to understand when you appear to refuse our requests. Fill us with your love and show us how to love. Enable us to understand your love for us, especially when we are in difficult situations. We ask this in the name of Jesus, who taught us how to pray. Amen.

37

So whatever you wish that men would do to you, do so to them; for this is the law and the prophets.

Chapter 7:12

J esus (or Matthew) deliberately associates the Father's providential care, as described in the previous saying, with the golden rule of human behaviour. He reminds us that the whole of the Jewish law and all the words of the prophets are directed towards this end. If we pray ardently and have faith in God's love and at the same time really try to love our neighbour, then we are on the path that leads to heaven.

Suppose a man begins to steal. He may find that this is an easy way to have a comfortable life in the material sense, until he is caught. How can this man be persuaded that it is wrong to steal because that is not what he would wish other people to do to him? There is the possibly apocryphal story of the burglar whose own house was burgled. He was ten times more indignant than the average person who is the victim of burglary. Before he himself became the victim he could not imagine what it was like to have strange hands rooting all through his house. Imagination is needed for a person to see the other person's viewpoint, unless experience is going to take a hand. However, it wouldn't be practical to make sure that every burglar has his own house burgled. Perhaps the way to get this important message through to people is by good moral education at the right stage of development.

The Jewish law or Torah was seen as a gift from God, transmitted through prophets, priests and teachers. God's servant, according to Second Isaiah, would bring God's law:

"He will not fail or be discouraged till he has established justice in the earth; and the coastlands wait for his law" (Isaiah 42:4).

The first five books of the Bible contain a number of law codes produced at different times. In the Books of Deuteronomy and Leviticus these are extensive. Quite often Jewish people refer to the Pentateuch as the Torah, though there is a sense in which the whole of the Jewish Bible or Old Testament is sometimes regarded as the Torah. When Jesus came to comment on the true law he summarized it as the law of love. It seems that lawyers and other people were aware of the summary of the law as recommended by Jesus (see Luke 10:27), but Jesus gave a whole new light to the law of love in his teaching and in his life. One of the parables which has had the greatest impact in this respect is the one about the Good Samaritan (Luke 10:30-37). Of course, we should never forget that the two laws which Jesus used to summarize the whole of Jewish law are to be found in the Pentateuch (see Deuteronomy 6:4-5 and Leviticus 19:18).

The Jewish prophets are often dismissed as people who prophesied only doom and judgement. What such critics forget is that some of the prophets were essentially preaching God's love and salvation and, indeed, it is possible to find strands of teaching about hope and love in the works of all the main prophets. One of the prophets who came to understand God's love in a very personal way was Hosea. Through his relationship with his unfaithful wife, to whom he remained constant, he perceived that God's love for Israel was a never failing and forgiving love. Second Isaiah (Isaiah 40-55) was supremely a prophet of salvation and hope. He prophesied the return of the Israelites to the land from which they had been exiled. He was also very eloquent about God's forgiving love:

...let the wicked forsake his way, and the unrighteous man his thoughts; let him return to the Lord, that he may have mercy on him, and to our God, for he will abundantly pardon (Isaiah 55:7).

The true thread of Jewish prophecy was constantly seeking

125

to understand God's nature, and even the doleful Jeremiah discovered that he was confronted by a forgiving and loving God (see Jeremiah 31:34).

What Jesus showed his own and subsequent generations is that it is all too easy to bury the true spirit of the law and the prophets under a mass of silly rules and regulations. We can fall into this trap today if we are not watchful and we can become obsessed with minor Church matters. However, the teaching of Jesus is a wonderful corrective and helps us to adjust our sights to the true ideal world of God's providential care and love. When we feel God's kingdom growing within ourselves, we can begin to understand what God's love is all about. Perhaps we are then more able to try to practise what Jesus preached.

Bible readings

Psalm 119:121-128; John 15:1-11; Galatians 5:22-26.

Prayer

O Lord, please help us to understand the teaching of Jesus, not only in our minds, but also in our hearts. Fill us with your love so that we may try to love others as we ourselves would wish to be loved. Help us to understand the true spirit of the law and the prophets, that we may the better understand the Bible as your revelation and may your Holy Spirit guide us in our study of your word. Amen.

38

Enter by the narrow gate; for the gate is wide and the way is easy, that leads to destruction, and those who enter by it are many. For the gate is narrow and the way is hard, that leads to life, and those who find it are few.

Chapter 7:13-14

It is discouraging to be told that only a few people can find the way to life. The Greek word for "life" used here often refers to "eternal life" or the "life of the kingdom of God" and this seems to be what Jesus means. The symbolism of the two gates is very effective. Most people go through the wrong gate at some point in their lives because it gives such easy entry. It is a natural human tendency to avoid the difficult route through the narrow gate. For example, the student who hopes to graduate eventually may be tempted to socialise a lot because it is pleasant. There may even be the temptation to take drugs because it seems like the thing to do. When the time comes to revise for examinations the student just can't get round to doing any work, not anyway until it is almost too late. The wide gate to destruction has been all too tempting and the narrow gate seems very difficult to enter. That sort of situation often happens to people and the right action can be very hard to take. If this was the only saying in the Bible on the subject of going to heaven we should have to rate our chances of getting there as being very low indeed.

If we try to interpret the saying in relation to our present lives we are then led to ask what the word "life" might mean. The word sometimes refers to that quality of life which is enlightened by God's grace, that is, a life lived with the Holy Spirit as a constant companion. This is a gift from God and it is a very wonderful gift which is offered freely. The difficulty is that acceptance of the gift entails the acceptance of responsibility. At certain stages in their lives some people may not wish to accept such responsibility. The temptations to go in other directions are many. Following these other directions may well lead to disaster, the sort of unhappy outcome which results from leading a selfish life based on pursuit of pleasure without regard for other people. The girl who sleeps around may lose the respect of the men she knows. She may be led into prostitution. Then, when it is almost too late she discovers she has wasted half of her life. That is when the old proverb about it "never being too late" can be of real value. It is never too late to turn to God.

The entry by the narrow gate may then refer to the kind of discipline which the committed person has to follow, including regular prayer and worship, studying the Bible and the faith, sharing our resources, thinking seriously about moral issues, trying to help others in difficulty and keeping to Christian principles in all we do. People may try several times before finding the right gateway. The wonderful thing about Christianity is that another chance is always on offer.

There is another side to the coin, which is the wonderful adventure of being a follower of Christ. The underlying discipline enables people to do much more with their time and talents than they would otherwise be able to do. There is the sense of purpose and the satisfaction of trying to love and serve God and our neighbour. The way to life is richly rewarding. While it is hard to enter the narrow gate initially, the pathway it leads to is a very happy one in ultimate terms. If, on the other hand, we go through the wider gate and follow our own selfish impulses, the ultimate result may be a very unhappy one.

There is another dimension to this saying. If we are searching for the right way to go, without help and only using our own resources, it may very well be difficult to find the way to life. The fact is, however, that many people are searching and those who have already found the right direction are always ready to help those who are still trying to find their bearings. Further, and probably more importantly, if we are prepared to ask God for guidance we are much more likely to find the right way forward. We are not left to our own devices. God has clearly revealed himself to the world and has opened ways of communication between heaven and earth. Those who turn to Christ will sooner or later find the narrow gate, though there may be difficulties on the way. The saying perhaps serves to remind us that even the Christian life is not all roses and sunshine. Even so, perhaps it is worth remarking that it is the first step in the Christian life that is the most difficult. After that first step we have a companion, Our Lord himself.

Bible readings

Psalm 16; Luke 1:67-79; Hebrews 12:12-24.

Prayer

O Lord, show us the true path that leads to life and prevent us from following the many wrong paths which may lie before us. Help us to learn both the discipline and the joy of being a follower of your Son, Jesus Christ. And guide us by your Holy Spirit throughout our lives so that we may finally enter into the eternal life of your glorious kingdom. Amen.

39

Beware of false prophets, who come to you in sheep's clothing but inwardly are ravenous wolves. You will know them by their fruits. Are grapes gathered from thorns, or figs from thistles? So, every sound tree bears good fruit, but the bad tree bears evil fruit. A sound tree cannot bear evil fruit, nor can a bad tree bear good fruit. Every tree that does not bear good fruit is cut down and thrown into the fire. Thus you will know them by their fruits.

Chapter 7:15-20

T his saying advises us that we ought not to judge people at their face value, nor at the value they place upon themselves when in the public eye. Yet again, Jesus is tearing aside the veil of hypocrisy which was to be found among his critics. Of course, we are all in danger of becoming hypocrites and perhaps we show one side of ourselves to the world at large while our families see another side of our characters. What we cannot do, however, is hide our true selves from God. Moreover, the actions we perform will ultimately show what kind of people we are. The fruits we bear will speak for themselves. In a very hard hitting passage St Paul contrasts the works of the flesh with the fruits of the spirit. The positive side of this comparison is as follows:

But the fruit of the spirit is love, joy, peace, patience, kindness, goodness, faithfulness, gentleness, self control... (Galatians 5:22).

The negative aspects of the comparison include, for example, "enmity, strife, jealousy, selfishness, dissension, party spirit, envy...", and that is less than half of Paul's list (see Galatians 5:19-21).

It would be impossible to categorize people with certainty to say each of us was a completely good tree or a completely bad tree. With the majority of people there are good qualities and bad qualities in their characters. As people become older the picture becomes clearer. Sometimes it is possible to see that a person has done evil deeds and sometimes that a person has done many good deeds. However, to place each type firmly in a category would have its dangers, at any rate by the criteria of human judgement. A person who has taken the wrong direction may turn round and take a better direction. For example, the convicted criminal may reform and become a model citizen and, in any case, he may well be a loving husband and father. A person who has done many good deeds may at the same time have a flaw in his character. For example, the head teacher who has done wonderful work in the local community may get into financial difficulties and start to "borrow" from the school fund.

Jesus deliberately paints a black and white picture in order to make his point clearer. He uses symbolism from everyday life in the country, a symbolism that everyone would readily understand. The gardener knows that if a bush or tree is diseased very badly it has to be removed and destroyed. He also knows that if he allows weeds to grow in his garden he is not going to get apples or pears from them. If he wants a good crop he needs to choose sound trees and then to look after them properly. There is a potential judgement underlying the imagery. Ultimately, if a person allows his life to become very badly disordered in the moral sense he will have to pay the price. The price may be paid in this life in terms of guilt and unhappiness. But even if someone appears to escape the consequences of his evil deeds in this life, the moral law that lies behind all existence will not be denied. The day of judgement cannot be avoided.

It is interesting that the Greek version of Jesus's saying uses the word "prophet" prefixed by the Greek word "pseudo-". We all know what "pseudo" means because it is a common word in our vocabulary. The same word in Greek is used to describe a liar. Jesus is saying, then, that we sometimes have to beware of people who deliberately stand in the public view as preachers or prophets. They may turn out to be liars or cheats. Of course, we do not always have the wisdom to know when a person is using deceptive words. Such a person may have convinced himself that what he is doing or saying is right and good and true.

We are warned in the third of the Mosaic commandments that we should not take the name of the Lord in vain. If our deeds do not match our words we may, in fact, be breaking that commandment without realising it. If we go to church on Sunday and indicate that we accept the words and moral principles that lie behind the service, and then go home and behave in a way which contradicts what we have stated either explicitly or implicitly in church, then we are in effect breaking the third commandment. The prophet Amos recognized clearly that our worship and our ethics should go together. He wrote:

> Seek good, and not evil, that you may live; and so the Lord, the God of hosts, will be with you (Amos 5:14).

Bible Readings

Psalm 15; John 8:31-47; 1 Corinthians 5:6-8.

Prayer

O Father of all truth, place in our hearts the spirit of truth so that all we do or say may be in accord with your will. Cleanse our hearts from all mischief and falsehood so that we may bear good fruit rather than evil fruit. Go before us always so that on the great day of judgement we may not be ashamed to kneel before you. In the name of Jesus Christ, our Lord. Amen.

40

Not every one who says to me, "Lord, Lord," shall enter the kingdom of heaven, but he who does the will of my Father who is in heaven. On that day many will say to me, "Lord, Lord, did we not prophesy in your name, and cast out demons in your name, and do many mighty works in your name?" And then I will declare to them, "I never knew you; depart from me, you evil doers."

Chapter 7:21-23

Those who address God in prayer are not necessarily doing so in a way that is acceptable to God. This, of course, is a warning to all of us and it is a continuation of the previous sayings concerning hypocrisy. Only if we do the will of the Father shall we be acceptable on the Day of the Lord. "That day" is a technical expression for the day when Christ will come in power and judgement. The phrase is frequently used in the Old Testament in a similar context. For example, the prophet Zechariah writes:

> On that day there shall be a fountain opened for the house of David and the inhabitants of Jerusalem to cleanse them from sin and uncleanness (Zechariah 13:1).

Jesus indicates that when that day comes he will be make himself known to each of us. If our claims to have been good stewards are spurious, he will refuse to accept us.

It is not easy in specific situations to know what God's will is. However, in the general sense it is clear that God wishes us to order our lives in accord with the teachings of Jesus. Love of God and sincere love for our neighbour are two principles which Jesus gave us to follow. While we could multiply examples of how we apply these two rules,

Jesus always points to the spirit behind our actions as the important factor in what we do. In the general sense, then, Christians should be clear as to what is expected of them by following the teachings of Jesus.

But how can we know God's will in particular situations? If the answer to a problem is not clear we obviously need to think about the various dimensions of the problem. Many pastors would suggest that prayers for guidance are the best way forward. However, along with such prayer we ought to use the faculties that God has given us to try to think our way through. Special guidance may or may not be given. The Holy Spirit is sometimes silent, but at other times he chooses to give signposts, perhaps through people we talk to or through books we read. If we do not take the trouble to seek God's will, not only will our lives be disordered, but we shall also find it difficult to face Christ when "that day" comes.

Ignatius Loyola, founder of the Jesuits in the sixteenth century, used to follow a definite method in order to find God's will. First he would pray for guidance. Then he would think out carefully the different aspects of his problem, writing down the pros and cons. Finally, he would make a rational decision, offering this to God in prayer. When trying to solve a difficult problem this sounds like a sensible way forward.

Three kinds of activity, followed supposedly in Jesus's name, are listed in the saying of Jesus above: prophesying, casting out demons and doing mighty works. Presumably these do not make up an exhaustive list. However, it can be imagined that a person might prophesy or preach in the name of Jesus while at the same time missing the point of the whole exercise. In his great hymn to love, Paul sees clearly that prophecy without love is of little value:

And if I have prophetic powers and understand all mysteries and all knowledge, and if I have all faith, so as to remove mountains, but have not love, I am nothing (1 Corinthians 13:2).

134

The idea of casting out demons as a religious activity causes difficulty for some people. It is essentially a question of how to label a serious spiritual or mental disorder. Some people would prefer to use modern psychological terms, rather than the vocabulary of demonology. Jesus seems to imply that some people might attempt to cast out demons without his blessing. Again, wrong motivation could be the reason for our Lord's rejection of such acts. Interestingly enough, Luke's Gospel quotes Jesus as giving a slightly different view:

> John answered, "Master, we saw a man casting out demons in your name, and we forbade him, because he does not follow with us." But Jesus said to him, "Do not forbid him; for he that is not against you is for you" (Luke 9:49-50).

The only logical conclusion is that Christ will give his blessing to people who have genuine care and love at the heart of their attempts to heal others.

With regard to the third activity, it is difficult to imagine that anyone could do mighty works without God's involvement. It may be that Jesus is referring to people who claim the credit for bringing about such events or who perhaps accept undeserved rewards. Perhaps Simon the "magician" described in Chapter 8 of the book of Acts is an example of a person with the wrong attitude in this respect. He had a reputation as a miracle worker before he met the Christian apostles, but when he saw what they did in the name of Christ he coveted their gift and offered payment for their secret. He was given short shrift by Peter (see Acts 8:9-24).

Any statement of Jesus must, of course, be taken in the context of the whole of his teaching and in the light of the New Testament as a whole. Repentant sinners, we are told, are not turned away. Indeed, the atoning work of Jesus was directed towards saving the whole world from sin. Consequently, while all of us may well face the day of judgement with fear and trembling, we have the assurance of Christ that he will be standing beside us at the judgement seat. That is one aspect of the Christian hope. As H.W. Baker puts it in a well known hymn:

In every time of need,
Before the judgement-throne,
Thy works, O Lamb of God, I'll plead,
Thy merits, not my own.

Bible readings

Psalm 143:1-10; 1 Thessalonians 5:1-22; Romans 8:1-11.

Prayer

O Lord, our Father and Preserver, give us the wisdom to know your will and the determination to carry it through in our daily lives. If we are ever lost or in danger of slipping on a dangerous pathway, guide us so that we know what would be pleasing to you. Help us to grow in the spiritual life so that we do not become complacent or hypocritical. We ask these things, O Lord, through Jesus Christ, your Son, and through your most Holy Spirit. Amen.

41

Every one then who hears these words of mine and does them will be like a wise man who built his house upon the rock; and the rain fell, and the floods came, and the winds blew and beat upon that house, but it did not fall, because it had been founded on the rock. And every one who hears these words of mine and does not do them will be like a foolish man who built his house upon the sand; and the rain fell, and the floods came, and the winds blew and beat against that house, and it fell; and great was the fall of it.

Chapter 7:24-27

This parable makes an appropriate conclusion to the Sermon. It is an unforgettable story and it is easy for a person of any culture and of any age from about five upwards to understand. That is the beauty of many of the parables of Jesus. They are at the same time both profound and simple. The essential meaning is that a life based on the moral principles in the Sermon will be stable and will not disintegrate, whereas a life which is not so based will eventually collapse because it has no real foundation.

We all know that some people who are not Christians nevertheless try to base their lives upon good moral foundations. Some such people have a different kind of faith in God and some are agnostic. They are following the right pathway and their lives will have a measure of stability. However, the Christian is in a different position because not only is his life based on the teaching of Jesus, but he also has Jesus as a personal friend to rely upon in times of trial and tribulation.

Of course, all of us, including those who are Christians, are subject to temptations of many kinds. We can set off on the right road and then we can take the wrong turning. In most cases, when we do go wrong, it is because we have not kept to the Christian principles we have been taught.

The seven deadly sins (pride, covetousness, lust, envy, gluttony, anger, sloth) were defined many centuries ago and they are still as deadly today, with the added complication of more sophisticated temptations. Drug trafficking, the sale of pornographic videos, drunken driving, cheating on the stock market and breaking into computer systems are but a few of the modern versions of sin. A little thought actually shows that the "old fashioned" sins are often at the basis of these modern misdemeanours.

Some of us, when we do realise we have gone wrong, may take the opportunity to go back to square one so that we can start again. In Christian terms this is the result of repentance. Such repentance may indeed have to be very regular, but if we turn again to Christ and his teachings we can once again base our lives on firm foundations.

In this parable Jesus is taking two very traditional categories in Hebrew teaching, that is, the wise man and the foolish man. Indeed, wisdom teaching using these categories goes back to ancient Egypt and Babylon in its origins. The compiler of the Book of Proverbs writes of wisdom:

> My son, keep my words and treasure up my commandments with you; keep my commandments and live, keep my teachings as the apple of your eye...
> (Proverbs 7:1-2).

Of folly the Book of Proverbs says:

> Let not your heart turn aside to her ways, do not stray into her paths; for many a victim has she laid low...
> (Proverbs 7:25-26).

It is clear that as a teacher Jesus was operating in a very ancient and noble tradition.

Life can have its difficulties, as we all know, and sometimes these difficulties are not caused by ourselves. For example, inflation can bring financial difficulties for many people. Illness or bereavement may necessitate a different

138

kind of life style. Redundancy can cause acute domestic problems for the whole family. But if we abide in Christ such difficulties are placed in perspective, and if we are trying our best to live by Jesus's teaching with the help of the Holy Spirit, then with God's help we can withstand any storms that may assail us.

As Augustus Toplady's great hymn says:

Rock of ages, cleft for me,
Let me hide myself in thee...

The parable does make the same very important point. Rain, floods and winds may come, but the house we are in the process of building will stand if we listen to the wisdom of Christ.

Bible readings

Psalm 31:1-5; James 3:13-18; 1 Corinthians 1:18-25.

Prayer

O Father of all wisdom, help us to build strong lives on the foundations of Christ. Help us to avoid foolish paths and to resist the many temptations that assail us. Grant us the power of your Holy Spirit that we may withstand all the storms of this life, so that we may at last reach the still waters of your peace in heaven. We ask this in the name of Jesus the Lord. Amen.

42

And when Jesus finished these sayings, the crowds were astonished at his teaching. For he taught them as one who had authority, and not as their scribes.

Chapter 7:28-29

I t is not surprising that the people were astonished at the teaching of Jesus. Quite often he seemed to be turning things upside down. His treatment of the revered Ten Commandments, for example, was so radical that he completely changed the perspective of his listeners, but nevertheless made the rules so personal that his interpretation was much more severe than the traditional one given by the scribes. Moreover, he did this with the authority of one who was absolutely certain of his ground, with an authority which seemed to have the divine blessing. This is deliberately emphasised by Matthew in the following chapter. The centurion comes to Jesus for help on account of a sick servant. Jesus offers to come and heal the servant, but the centurion says that he himself, as a centurion, is a man of authority and he understands the authority that Jesus has. All Jesus has to do is give the word and the servant will be healed. Impressed by the man's faith, Jesus does give the authoritative word and the servant is healed "at that very moment" (see Matthew 8:5-13).

Of course, in retrospect we can see that Jesus not only had the divine blessing, but that he was speaking as God's Son. This was not apparent to his listeners. They did speculate as to who he was. They could see him as a prophet or even as a Messiah. But the Jews had sometimes seen then, and have sometimes seen since, a range of people as Messiahs. The idea that Jesus could be God's Son was not understood until after the resurrection, and even then it took quite a lot of thinking by people like St Paul to work out the implications of this idea. To be sure, there is still speculation about Jesus and who he was, and some people today regard him simply as a good teacher, while others pour scorn on the idea that he might have been the Son of God. Yet, whatever attacks are made on Jesus and the Gospel, the pages of the New Testament speak with an authenticity which cannot be gainsaid. Moreover, the reality of Christ as the Son of God is not confined to the pages of the Bible. He is a living reality.

The kind of authority which teachers in the time of Jesus relied upon was tradition. If a moral precept or a theological idea was based on the writings or oral teachings of great men of the past, then it was regarded as authoritative. The law and the prophets were standard references. To some extent, of course, we do that today. We like to quote so called "authorities" when we produce scholarly works or sermons. Just occasionally a truly original thinker appears and ideas have to change.

In modern times, Teilhard de Chardin and Charles Darwin, for example, could be placed in that category. Some of the Old Testament prophets were either original thinkers or they were inspired by God, depending on which viewpoint is preferred. They changed the current ideas of their time, but then in their turn became part of tradition. A good example perhaps is the prophet Amos. He changed the concept of the Day of the Lord from an over optimistic belief in God's saving help in all circumstances, to one of God's impending judgement. It would be a day "of darkness, and not light" (see Amos 5:18-20). During the following centuries Amos's original view became standardised. However, in the case of the Sermon on the Mount, we have a body of teaching which is always radical, because it always challenges preconceptions and pretensions.

The danger with radical teaching, as found in the Sermon on the Mount, is that we might not read it carefully enough because it has so long been accepted as a standard code of ethics and belief. However, this collection of sayings will never lose its true force if people are prepared to approach it without preconceptions. Many parts of the Bible reveal new treasures each time we read them. Thoughtful reading brings new insights. This is not surprising if the Bible is a divinely inspired book. Of course, the exact nature of the authority of the Bible is disputed. However, at the very least most Christians would agree that the writers of the various books of the Bible had a deep experience of God. Consequently, whatever view Christians take of verbal inspiration, most would accept that the Bible is God's word in some sense.

If Jesus was the Son of God, as we believe, his expression of his experience during his incarnation must always have divine authority. This applies not only to his saving work on the cross, but also applies to his teaching. As a human being Jesus was given special insights and his authority will always be preeminent in Christian circles. The Sermon on the Mount will always have a special authority in the Church because, along with the parables, it constitutes the greatest collection of sayings that any teacher has ever bestowed upon his disciples.

Bible readings

Jeremiah 1:4-10; Luke 20:1-8; Matthew 28:16-20.

Prayer

O Father, we give you thanks for the revelation of your word in the Bible. Especially we thank you for the teaching of Jesus and we pray that we may acquire the discipline of study and the wisdom of interpretation so that we may understand your word more clearly. May your word indeed be a lamp unto our feet so that we may find our way forward when the world seems dark. We ask this in the name of Jesus Christ, your Son. Amen.